Looking at Sails

Looking at Sails

Dick Kenny

Second Edition

Illustrated by Peter Campbell

Photographs by Dave Blunden and Others

ISBN 0-87742-976-6

Published by International Marine Publishing Company
P.O. Box 220
Camden, Maine 04843
(207) 236-4837

Filmset in Great Britain
Printed in Italy

Contents

Foreword

The years since 1978, when Bruce Banks and I wrote the original *Looking at Sails,* have witnessed a remarkable surge in the development of sails and sailmaking. Sadly Bruce is no longer here to record them. His influence on that edition, both as master sailmaker and sailor, was total. My pleasant role was simply to sit at his knee and listen as the story unravelled.

To attempt therefore to bring that book up to date, without Bruce's unique talent and experience, was I considered a thankless task; and the decision was made to start afresh. To help, in place of one man, I would enlist the expertise of the best specialists I could get on each aspect of the subject. It has proved a fascinating experience.

My thanks therefore to Dr. John Wellicome of the University of Southampton for his patience on the mysteries of hydro and aerodynamics; Mike Sandman, John Sparkman Jnr. and Mark Spruce of Bainbridge for so enthusiastically sharing their knowledge of sailcloth design and manufacture; and both Peter Kay of North Sails, and Bill Rogers of Sobstad for their help in my understanding of the rapidly changing world of sail design.

Both Bryan Axford and Bob Lankester of Hood Sailmakers were generous with their time and that of their loft, as was Ken Rose for the original edition, and Bruce's son David, now running Bruce Banks Sails.

I was particularly grateful to Titch and Tony Blachford for the day they put themselves and their yacht *Smokey III* at our disposal, as I was to Blake Simms for *Hurricane Tree*, Roger Eglin for *Fruesli II*, and the crew of my own *Red Otter* for their help with the photography.

Photographing sails against the ever changing moods of the sky is not an easy task and Dave Blunden achieved remarkable results. Most of the rig, and many of the boat pictures in the following pages were his; supplemented with some outstanding photography from around the world from the Barry Pickthall Picture Library (PPL), Colloryan and North Sails Inc., courtesy of Dave Delembar.

The presentation of the book, and all of the illustrations were the talented work of Peter Campbell, assisted by Rob Burt. My grateful thanks go to them for lightening the load, as they do to Diana Hirst for transforming indecipherable scribble into immaculate typescript.

The end result is dedicated to the memory of Bruce Banks.

D.K.
Maidenhead 1987

Introduction

'Only sails drive the boat forward; everything else is holding it back.' The words belong to the late Bruce Banks, and while a pure physicist might be inclined to fine tune their directness, to most sailors they capture the subject in a nutshell.

To a landsman, unconcerned with the mysteries of why a boat can sail towards the wind, or indeed why some sail faster than others with the wind behind them, the answer is simple. Offer a large enough surface to a strong enough wind, and it will bowl you along, if not over.

Every sailor knows there is more to it than that. The very first lesson, learned before even stepping into a boat, is that with sails sheeted in, it can be driven against the force of the wind.

Sadly the search for knowledge, in many cases, stops right there. Accepting that the principle works, too many sailors appear content to pay scant attention to getting the best from their vessels' 'engine'.

At the other end of the spectrum sits the keen racer who understands well the vital role being played out aloft between wind and fabric. Ironically it is the latter who highlights the lack of absolute answers. The sailor, content to leave sails well alone as long as they work, can remain blissfully ignorant of such exotica as finite element analysis of membrane structures, while the sun sinks slowly in the west. For the racing sailor on the other hand, every avenue leading to that extra tenth of a knot has to be explored. Yet each new piece of jigsaw added to the understanding, in turn, raises yet more questions to be answered. Even the experts—the sailmakers, who design and shape sails and who understand best of all how and why they work, will all admit they have still some way to go along the road from art to finite science.

The beginnings

It is always interesting to wonder why something first happened. To most tastes, meat and potatoes are more palatable once cooked; but who on earth first discovered that throwing one's dinner into the fire improved the eventual eating.

Speculating about the origins of sail entails a less imaginative leap. Picture some nameless but overtired fisherman, back in the mists of time. Having paddled further than usual in search of his catch, he takes off his animal skin, attaches one end to an oar held high, and the wind wafts him home in time for tea. Animal skins being size limited, the Mk II version had to await a material breakthrough.

It came in the shape of woven cloth; but remember it was still only a one-way downwind ticket. This state of the art must have lasted until the turn of the millennium, because we know that until then, the substitution of a few hundred slaves was relied upon to take a vessel to windward.

The secret was nevertheless already there. As sails grew in area, so the centre bulged before the weight of the wind. Slowly it must have dawned that the boats went faster if this sail was angled across the wind, and then that if the edge of the sail was pointed far enough forward the vessel defied all known logic and went to windward. The aerofoil had been discovered.

Early square-rigs were used only before the wind. *Courtesy: BLA Publishing Ltd.*

photo: Colloryan

Bernoulli

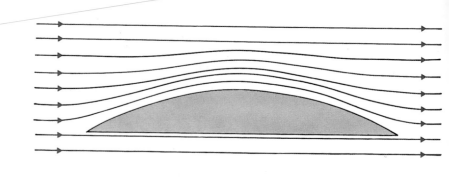

It took Professor Daniel Bernoulli in 1738 to turn this practice into theory and then Law. In a nutshell, he established that for any fluid, pressure plus velocity (speed) is a constant. Consequently if a fluid—and air is a fluid—moves faster, then pressure is reduced; and if it slows down, pressure is increased.

For simplicity's sake at this stage imagine the wind as a series of parallel straight lines into the path of which is introduced a rigid aerofoil shape roughly similar to the cross section of a sail, or an aeroplane wing. As the wind arrives at the leading edge it splits. That forced over the upper curved surface is compressed between the obstruction—or aerofoil—and the undisturbed straight lines of flow above. This compression accelerates the flow in line with Venturi's Law, and in doing so reduces its pressure. In other words a partial vacuum is formed, up into which the aerofoil is sucked. That is the much simplified explanation of lift.

To demonstrate the idea physically, hold a tablespoon lightly between finger and thumb with the curved back of the spoon close to running water. As the curved surface touches the stream of water, a jerk will be felt as the spoon is sucked into the flow. To anyone unfamiliar with the principles of science this may not appear overconvincing. However the lift generated over an aerofoil, according to this law, is quite sufficient to hold a 350 ton jumbo jet in the sky.

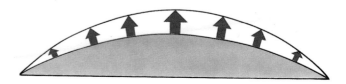

While the above is over-simplistic an early glimpse points more clearly the way in which sails for the modern yacht have developed.

Below the waterline

How this lift is harnessed into windward movement calls for an understanding of the same fluid dynamics, but this time below the surface as well as above.

A very basic illustration of how lift (red arrows) is generated over a curved surface.

As the curved spoon back touches the flow (right), it is sucked into it.

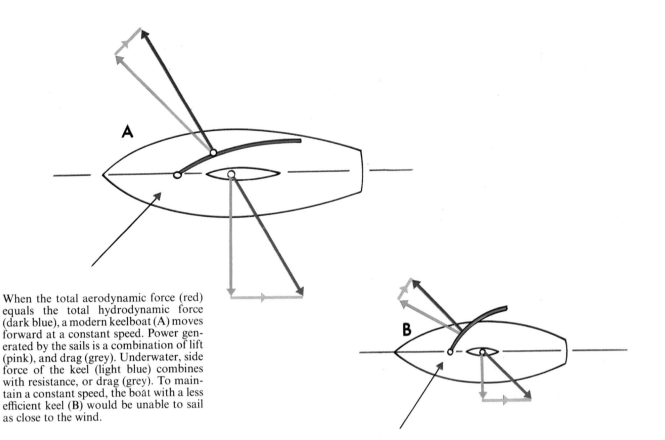

When the total aerodynamic force (red) equals the total hydrodynamic force (dark blue), a modern keelboat (A) moves forward at a constant speed. Power generated by the sails is a combination of lift (pink), and drag (grey). Underwater, side force of the keel (light blue) combines with resistance, or drag (grey). To maintain a constant speed, the boat with a less efficient keel (B) would be unable to sail as close to the wind.

The early nineteenth century saw the apogee of the sailing man-of-war. It was however very short lived. Thirty years after the Battle of Trafalgar, those very same vessels were being fitted with steam engines. The reason, pure and simple, was that however majestic they might be, they went to windward like a sack of potatoes. The problem lay below the waterline, where the lack of a hydrodynamic keel, balancing the force of the wind across the sails, prohibited the latter being sheeted in closely enough to generate forward lift. It was the addition of such a keel, following on Newton's Theory that every action must have an equal and opposite reaction,

which led to sails really being put to work to windward i.e. set fore and aft.

On a modern yacht, hydrodynamic force on the keel going through the water has to balance the aerodynamic force generated by the wind over the sail. In the illustration these two forces are split into their two components. On the keel (or underwater section), the total force is broken down between side force perpendicular to the direction of travel and the resistance, or drag on the keel and hull hindering the boat's progress through the water. On the closehauled sail, angled to the wind, the countering forward force can be broken down be-

tween lift, perpendicular to the wind, and drag, parallel to it.

Not illustrated, but equally relevant, is the need to counter the heeling moment generated on the closehauled sail with an equal and opposite righting moment of the keel.

What becomes clear is the more efficient the side force of the keel in relation to hull and keel resistance, the closer to the wind the boat can be sailed.

It can also be seen that part of the sail force generated is in the form of drag. The relationship between sail lift and drag is fundamental to efficient sailing and this crucial element will be expanded upon later.

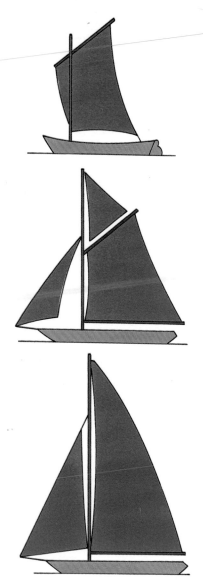

The early lugsail (top) was a forerunner of the gaff-rig (centre) to which was added a topsail. Both were combined to form the Marconi mainsail of today.

Before that however, a word or two on sails as they have developed today. The triangle-form bermudian mainsail rig is a relatively recent extension of the gaff mainsail plus topsail, which in turn developed from the dipping lugsail, one step removed from a

square sail hung from a yard. This evolution followed closely the developing understanding of underwater form allowing sails to be sheeted closer and closer to the centreline.

Edges

Interestingly the names still used aboard a modern yacht have their roots in the old square riggers. When attempting to beat, the windward leading edge of a square sail was led forward to a wooden turning block (the chess-trees) and sheeted tight. The area where the chess-trees were fixed was called the 'loof'. Hence luff, the leading edge of modern fore and aft sails.

The opposite of the loof, i.e. the edge of the squaresail furthest from the wind, down to leeward, was known as the lee edge, from which the modern leech derives.

The lower edge of the sail, the foot, holds no mysteries. It is now what it always has been.

Corners

Similarly the head needs no amplification other than to note that whereas once it described the whole length of the upper edge of the squaresail (and still does when correctly applied to a gaff rig mainsail), its status in the bermudian triangle has shrunk to the upper corner.

The tack on the other hand takes its name, at the forward lower corner of the sail, from the rope, or sheet, by which it was led and held forward and down.

Unfortunately the origins of the word clew, in the lower corner of the sail, either weather clew or

leeward-clew, depending on the ship's tack, defies research. It is merely a guess to suggest that somehow corner and lower became abbreviated aboard the ships of the time. Today it is exclusively used to describe the after corner of the sail.

Jib

Before leaving the past, a word about jibs. As will become clear, on today's fore and aft rig yacht they play a crucial—if not the crucial—role in driving the boat to windward. Long before their aerodynamic contribution was realised, fore and aft jibs were an integral part of the square rigged ship and her smaller sisters. Whether their sailors understood the contribution to forward drive made by the small fore and aft sail is debatable, but its value was certainly underlined by one naval historian writing in 1897.

'The jib, notwithstanding the fact that it is small and stands outboard, is a very important agent in sailing. It steadies the boat on her course, helps her round when she is put about, prevents her running suddenly up into the wind, and acts as a good guide to the helmsman, when sailing in the eye of the wind, for by its tendency to chaffer (or shiver) it tells him when he is sailing too close.' One hundred years on it is hard to find a word with which to argue.

The material

If, as speculated earlier, sailing evolved due to the inherent stretch of woven cloth, it is ironic that that same characteristic has proved the bane of every

sailmaker's working life ever since. Why not—one might ask— use a more stable and rigid material from which to derive power? An aircraft designer knows to a very high tolerance exactly what his aerofoil will do at a particular air speed, and once built it will stay in shape. Why not use aluminium for sails?

Well for a start, to match varying conditions every boat would carry dozens of them—one for every couple of knots extra wind speed, and for, say, every five degrees difference in the wind angle. To say nothing of where this cathedral of metal would be stowed.

Of course the prospect is too silly for words; but woven cloth has even more going for it than that.

Weight aloft is critical to any sailboat. Any excess that contributes to the heeling moment, unbalances the counter forces below the waterline—with a consequent erosion of the limited drive force available. Weight also increases the fore and aft pitching moment, thereby dramatically increasing the boat's hydrodynamic drag.

Even though it seems hard to believe, fabric sails are also cheaper: first to buy, and then to repair.

Above all these however is the fact that fabric sails are safer. In a building breeze, a jib can be changed for something smaller, and then smaller, until finally handed altogether. With fabric, this can be achieved without risking life and limb on a plunging foredeck. Similarly the mainsail

can be reefed to suit the conditions; in many cases these days without leaving the security of the cockpit.

Contrast this with the nearest equivalent—so far—to the metal sail hypothesis. A number of heavily sponsored multi-hulls have experimented in recent years with aerodynamically cross-sectioned and swivelling masts, sometimes five or six feet deep, extending back into where the luff of the mainsail would otherwise be. To date more than one sailor has

13

The area of this metal foil mast is roughly equal to that of the reefed mainsail. In a blow, the foil cannot be taken down.

Stars and Stripes to leeward of *Kookaburra*. The two boats, representing a multi-million dollar search for speed, battle it out in the 1987 America's Cup. *Photo: Nick Rains/ PPL*

wished, in a howling gale, that the foil area could be reduced. Usually just before disaster struck.

Peaceful backwater

Sails, for all their apparent progress, are still however a backwater. Ironically this has been highlighted in the past half dozen years by the accelerated search for finite answers. The America's Cup, and increasing professionalism/sponsorship at the sharp end of the sport, has produced money, enthusiasm and many technolog-

ical tools with which to work—and yet the answers are slow in coming.

Progress in sail development has in fact been incredibly slow, compared with, for example, aviation, its aerodynamic soul sister. Whereas the latter in three quarters of a century has travelled from six feet off the ground, to the moon and back, the former relatively speaking, has been in irons.

The reason is fairly obvious. The development of sails came to an end with a puff of steam in the mid 19th century. Progress since then into understanding why sails

work, and more importantly how to make them work better, has been borne on the shoulders of first, working sailors and latterly sportsmen, eager to outdo their fellows. Neither had, or have, deep pockets comparable to those of states racing for military might.

It is a fact that today almost all that is known about the effect of wind on sails derives from aircraft related aerodynamics. Similarly hull and keel forms are based on the results of hard won experience, and the fluid dynamics as applied to ships' bottoms.

Much of the aerodynamic knowledge is scaled down hypothesis. Engineers working in the wind tunnel have little interest in what happens to an aerofoil in under 30 knots, and even that once essential tool is past its prime, increasingly overtaken by the super-computer. Wondrous though their answers may be, programming in order to ask the question is astronomically expensive.

The amount of pure research into sail aerodynamics has been painfully small. Over twenty years ago C.A. 'Tony' Marchaj published the results of his work, in the now standard reference works, *Sailing Theory and Practice* and *Aero-hydrodynamics of Sailing*; work that has been continued, albeit spasmodically at Southampton University in England. But only recently a study to pin down pressure distribution on a sail—the stuff of life to a sail designer—foundered before completion through lack of funds.

On the other hand there is some good news. The computer, fed with the fruits of experience, is coming up with answers of its own; not only into why sails work, but in how to design, cut and shape cloth into forms that are themselves evolving. The intake however, still relies heavily on the sailor, combining all that is already known with practical experience, to lead the machine down the most productive avenues.

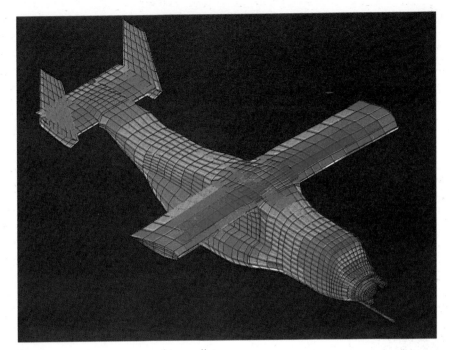

Super-computers programmed to predict pressure flows are a direct result of defence and civil aviation R&D programmes. This is the Boeing V-22 Osprey for the United States Forces.

With access to the same super-computers, Michael Richelsen of North Sails has applied the technology to sail flow analysis. *Photo: North Sails Inc.*

The theory

The simple explanation of how a curved surface introduced into an air (or fluid) flow produces lift is fine for the casually interested. For the sailor intent on understanding and maximising the power aloft, it very soon poses more questions than it answers. On the surface it would appear that by simply increasing the curve on the obstruction, more suction would be generated making the boat go faster—simple logic which any sailor knows soon runs out of steam. Again, the thickness of a sail, say 2 mm, is hardly comparable to that of an aeroplane wing as a lift generating obstruction. There is obviously more to this subject than meets the eye in that earlier, much simplified explanation. Unfortunately there is no halfway house in this understanding, and it is so basic to almost everything to do with how and why sails work that, even for the untechnically orientated, it is all or nothing.

First the concept of lift versus drag. In a given wind speed, if a boat is accelerating, the lift forces moving her forward must be greater than the drag forces pulling her back. The opposite is true when boat speed decays. At a constant speed through the water the lift and drag are both equal and opposite. In the case of a yacht this applies equally to the keel and the sails. Both are contributing both lift and drag as they interact with their respective fluids i.e. water for the keel and air

for the sails. The proportion of lift to drag generated by each is therefore fundamental to the effectiveness with which the boat can be driven forward.

So what are these opposing forces and how are they generated?

Lift

Consider first the example of a circular shape introduced into an air flow. Many use a ball as an example, but somewhat more graphic is the idea of a drop of water from a garden hose. Bernoulli's Law says that for any fluid—and remember air is a fluid—pressure plus speed is constant. Increase the speed and pressure drops; slow the speed and pressure rises.

The first effect that the air has on the circular water drop takes place on the mid-point of its forward edge. This is called the stagnation point where air flow speed across or around the drop is zero. Above and below that point the air separates around the water drop and as it does so has to accelerate across its surface. There are now two distinct forces acting on it. At the forward (stagnation) point velocity is at its lowest and therefore pressure highest, flattening its forward edge. Due to the accelerated airflow over its upper and lower surfaces, its top and bottom are at the same time being drawn into the lower pressure (higher speed) areas. Turning up the tap and increasing the speed of the water drop in relation to the air will result in these forces eventually pulling it apart into two finer droplets.

Interestingly, the direction in which this happens is the opposite to what one might expect. The top and bottom edges are drawn against the direction of movement due to the friction force between the air and droplet surface.

Air flow is generated around the water drop ejected by the hose (green). Pressure is highest at the leading edge stagnation point (X). Low pressure (red arrows) draws the drop apart. If hose velocity is increased (below) these pressures will actually pull the droplet apart (spray).

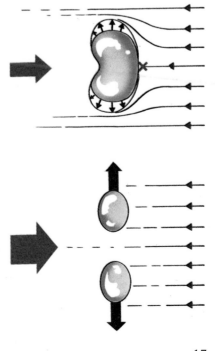

White Crusader off Perth. *Photo: Barry Pickthall*

Separation

To discover what happens to fluid flow when attempts are made to coax it around too sharp a curve, the example of a ball flying through the air is as good as any.

The flow, once parted at the stagnation point has decreased in pressure over the upper surfaces as it accelerates between the curve and the undisturbed airflow above. However, as it passes the apogee the constriction obviously decreases allowing the flow to decelerate to its original speed. Whilst the laws of physics provide that a fluid going from high pressure to low pressure will flow in a disciplined way, unfortunately from low to high pressure the opposite is true. It misbehaves. As soon as the pressure rises, the flow slows down, and separates. It is this separation, in a less extreme form than illustrated here, which every sailor has to guard against constantly when going to windward. It is the cause of both less lift, and increased drag, about which more later.

Boundary layer

There is also a frictional force between the obstruction and the fluid moving around it. This takes place in the area known as the boundary layer. Immediately next to the more solid surface there is a thin layer of the fluid which adheres itself and thereafter remains so. This thin layer moves at the same speed as the surface to which it is attached. The influence of the obstruction on the fluid progressively

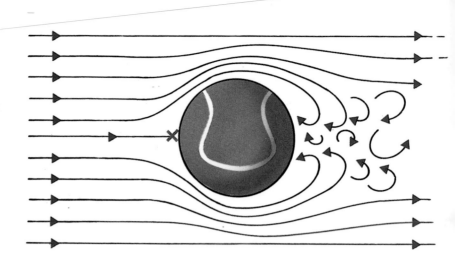

diminishes as the distance increases, until the boundary is reached where it no longer exerts any effect at all. Cake decoration provides a simple example. By drawing a knife across bands of contrasting colour lines of icing the frictional force against the surface of the knife is plainly seen, with its effect gradually decaying away. Air, which has a much higher viscosity will do the same, but to a much lesser degree. Both reactions can however be described as attached flow.

As pressure rises again behind the speeding ball (above), the flow separates into drag. (Below) The boundary layer effect magnified. Flow across the surface is slowed by friction. That immediately adjacent to the surface actually stops.

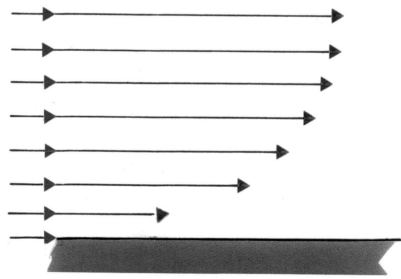

The knife drags the low viscosity icing within its boundary layer across the cake.

Turbulent vs laminar

The opposite of attached flow is separation. The often confused turbulent flow is in fact a subdivision of attached flow and not another word for separation.

Of the two types of attached flow, laminar is by far the most efficient. It depends on the flow lines staying in ranks like a well drilled regiment of soldiers wheeling around the parade ground, whilst its often maligned counterpart, turbulent flow, more resembles a queue of eager bargain hunters winding their way into the January sales; the elements are all bundled up together, but nevertheless all are moving in the same general direction.

In practice the efficiency advantages of laminar flow are probably of little relevance to the sailor due, on the one hand, to the relatively sharp angles around which the airflow has to be bent, and, on the other, the constant changes in speed as both sails and keel push through the waves.

Both remember, are terms for types of flow and it is keeping that attached which should remain the goal of the windward sailor.

Low to high pressure

Reverting for a moment to the boundary layer effect, it will be remembered that flow is slowed by the surface friction. In the example the surface was flat; but what happens within the boundary layer when a curved surface is introduced? As flow is compressed it speeds up; but once past the apogee it slows down again as pressure decreases. However the flow actually touching the surface is moving at the same speed as that surface. On a foil moving against the flow, for example, it would actually be travelling in the opposite direction.

This negative, or opposite, flow on the surface exerts an influence on that adjacent to it, by trying to turn it back upon itself. Obviously the slower that adjacent general flow is moving the better chance it has of succeeding.

Over the after surface of a shallow foil, flow is obviously decelerating less than over a deeper one and the chances of this separation, or misbehaviour are reduced. Increase the depth of camber, or the speed of the flow, and the differential within the boundary layer rises. Separation will now move rapidly forward to near the point where pressure starts building. From this point the foil is said to be stalled.

The foil now moving forward (top), turns the adjacent flow in the opposite direction. Over a more deeply curved foil, as below, the pressure and speed differential within the boundary layer is greater and separation much more likely.

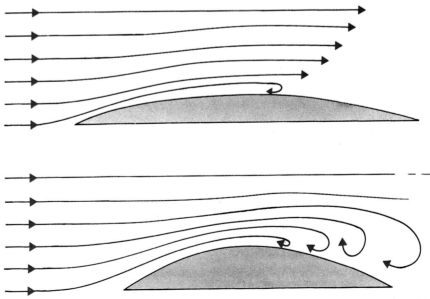

Angle of attack

The next stage in unravelling the mystery of how sails work calls for the introduction of a flat plate into the story. It is a fact of life that even a piece of plywood can generate enough lift to fly provided it is presented to the wind at the correct angle. Try manoeuvring one along the street in a gale.

Consider, with what has been said so far about speed and pressure, the flat plate shown here (A) angled to the wind at approximately that of a sail to windward.

The flow meets the plate slightly below its forward edge which becomes the stagnation point referred to earlier, i.e. the point of highest pressure. The flow above is forced up and around the leading edge, accelerating as it does so and dropping in pressure. From that point it gradually slows down again as the influence of the plate diminishes and the overall flow reasserts itself. The pressure rises again and of course flow going from low to high pressure misbehaves, and in this case separates almost at the leading edge. As flow first meets the board, that below the forward stagnation point is forced down the lower side of the plate, but when it reaches the rear edge, it turns the corner before continuing in its original direction. This

As the starting vortex in (C) is pushed aft, it sets up a general circular flow around the whole 'sail', and the stagnation points move counter-clockwise around to the leading and trailing edges. (1) shows the increase in flow velocity to leeward, and the decrease to windward, with the pressure differentials that result.

20

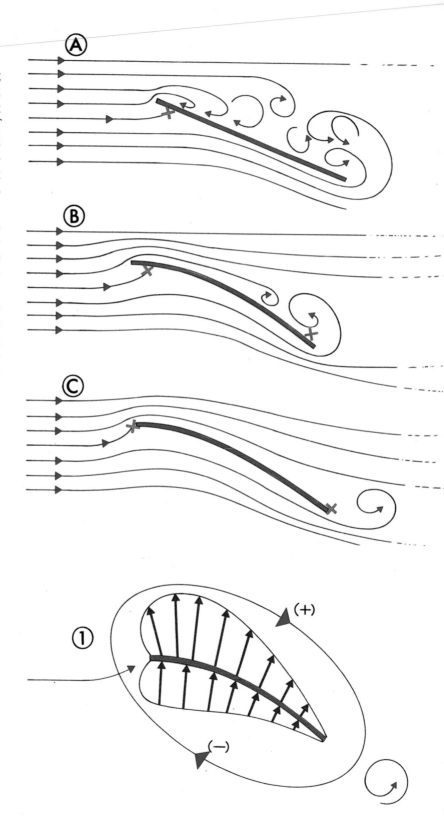

increase in speed lowers the pressure, and again as was seen with the ball earlier, low pressure to high pressure (on the leeward side) leads to gross misbehaviour. At last the end is in sight.

The sail as an aerofoil

By introducing a curve into the plate (B) this effect can be developed to the point where it means something to the sailor. The wind approaching at an angle similar to close-hauled meets the 'sail' at the stagnation point and separates. The upper flow is bent forward around the luff of the sail but, because it has to continue to accelerate over the leeward curve, is gently persuaded to follow that curve back along the sail. The flow remains attached within the boundary layer. On the lower (windward side) the flow travels aft; speeds up around the leech in an effort to revert to its original direction, but misbehaves into the low pressure area behind the leeward leech. Here another stagnation point develops and immediately a curling vortex of air develops. This is the starting vortex.

So far nothing has happened that is beyond fairly simple logic, but the next stage in the process is much harder to grasp, particularly for anyone untutored in the ways of physics. It is however the fulcrum upon which rests the complete theory. Remember, all that has happened so far equates to the moment the sail is sheeted into the wind.

As the starting vortex is formed, it is pushed by the general

The flow differentials on either side of this mainsail are clear, with the leeward reefing lines all streaming aft, and those to windward drooping in the reduced flow. *Photo: Colloryan.*

airflow past the leech into clean air (C). There, thanks to Newton's equal and opposite law, it starts a general airflow in the opposite direction, which grows to encompass the whole of the sail.

This is the difficult part to grasp. The general circulation generated by the vortex does not reverse the flow over the windward side of the sail. It relatively decreases that on the windward side and increases that on the leeward side. Both flows continue to move from forward to aft. One way of trying to grasp the idea is to think of someone on an early morning run around the decks of a cruise liner. Running towards the bow he will be approaching the next port of call faster than

21

when he turns and runs towards the stern. In the end however he will get there at the same time as the ship and everyone else.

On the sails, the general circulation slows down the flow on the windward side and accelerates the flow to leeward, and by so doing increases the pressure differential on either side. The result, as illustrated, is that the sail maintains the necessary aerofoil shape to generate lift.

Drag

The idea of general circulation having been established, now is a timely point at which to develop drag and its effect on the whole equation. Earlier references have been linked to the total force generated being the sum of lift and drag, its relevance being that the only lift to drive the boat forward is that remaining once the drag forces have been subtracted.

Pressure drag

Drag is formed when any obstruction is placed in a moving air or water flow. Sadly the shape with the highest drag ratio is one found only too readily on a boat. Any symmetrical or circular section such as wire, rod or rope rigging is the worst possible drag inducer. Reference to fig A will show why. The flow once past the mid point of any circular section separates into a confusion of spirals moving at high speeds relative to the surrounding airflow. High speed equals low pressure and this in team with the high pressure at the forward stagnation point combines to retard

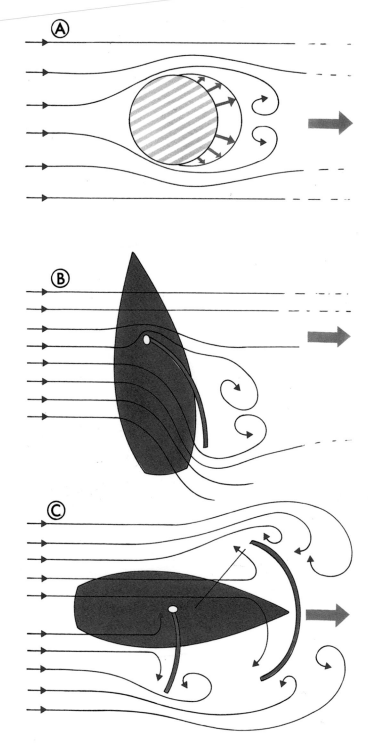

Three examples of pressure drag. (A) and (B) are bad. In (C), drag is working in the right direction, and pulls the spinnaker, and boat, forward.

22

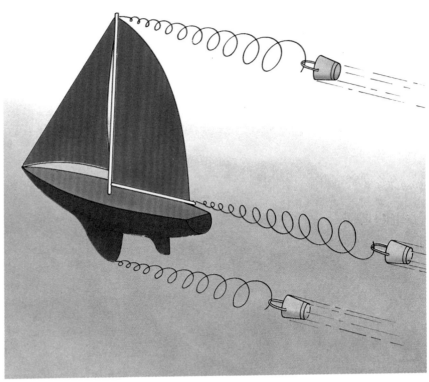

movement in that direction.

Even though a sail—or wing or keel—is asymmetrical and therefore producing lift, there is an important element of pressure drag also building up as the air, or water, flows past. Presenting the foil at either too great an angle to the flow, or with too deep a section will result in separation to a lesser or greater degree over the leeward surface, as described earlier.

This separation can happen as a result of the sail being too full for the wind strength, or as a result of poor trimming by the sailor, B. The most obvious example of the latter being sails too tightly sheeted on a reach, but sailing too far off, with sails hard in will have the same effect.

The swirling confused air in separated flow decreases pressure and retards forward movement. Of course such pressure drag is also displacing lift as it creeps forward so the effect is in a sense doubly detrimental. If allowed to continue the whole sail could end up being stalled. However, running off the wind, this is not quite the dragon it sounds. The force generated by a spinnaker on a run is almost totally pressure drag.

Viscous drag

The least of the three bogeys, viscous or friction drag, has a relatively minor role to play on sails, but more so on the keel. Air is five times less viscous than

water, and as the effect of viscous drag is basically to produce the aforementioned boundary layer it poses a more serious drawback to a dirty or unfair keel than it does to the minor irregularities in the average sail. Seams, stitches and creases all increase the friction drag but their contribution to total drag is not significant. In fact, when going to windward, both pressure and friction drag account for only around 25 per cent of this total.

Induced drag

The grand daddy of them all is induced drag. This is the drag caused directly by the process of generating lift with an asymmetrical shape. So far, the sail has only been considered in two di-

mensions. Its third dimension is its plan form with the head at the apex and foot at the bottom. It is in fact a sheet, separating high pressure air on one side, to windward, and low pressure on the opposite, to leeward. In doing so the sail is pushing against the high pressure, rather like an aircraft wing exerts a force equal to its weight on the air below it. This air naturally wishes to migrate out of the way, specifically towards the beckoning low pressure air on the opposite side of the foil. Where the two meet at the trailing edge or leech, a circular vortex is generated which spins outward towards the tip of the wing, or in the case of a sail, towards the head and clew. Once there it accelerates into an energy-sapping spiralling line-vortex. In the case of a jumbo jet these vortices can extend some 3 or 4 miles behind each wing tip. Luckily for the aircraft designer the fuselage forms an effective seal at the inboard end of the wing. The sails on a yacht are not so fortunate and tip vortices form both at the head and the foot of each sail, plus of course at the tip of the keel. To reduce the effect of drag, sail design, manufacture and trim all have a significant role to play. Suffice to leave them for the moment as a series of trailing buckets impeding the yacht's progress to windward.

Apparent wind

Finally, before completing the picture with the two sails interacting to windward, it is worth establishing the idea of apparent wind. To the sailor, and his sails, moving across the water, it is the only sort that really matters. True wind—or the wind that registers on a weathercock, firmly attached to a solid church steeple, has its place in the out and out sailboat racer's armoury; but only to calculate the apparent wind for the next leg of the course. Otherwise apparent is the one that counts.

The apparent wind speed and direction is that which is felt when moving. A boat motoring at 6 knots into a 10 knot breeze appears, to someone on board, to have 16 knots of wind over the deck—sixteen knots, that is of apparent wind. Motor in the opposite direction at six knots and the apparent wind drops to 4 knots. Motoring, or sailing, with the wind coming from any point other than ahead or directly astern, will not only give a different apparent speed, but will also alter the angle at which the airflow meets the boat. The apparent wind will also always come from an angle further forward than its true origin. Equally the faster the boat sails the further forward the direction moves and the faster—at least for winds forward of the beam—the speed appears.

If boat speed increases but wind remains constant, then apparent wind will increase and move forward, giving a header. If on the other hand boat speed remains constant but wind speed increases, the apparent wind will free.

These two rules have applications throughout the remainder of the book. They are therefore worth fixing in the mind.

Wind accelerating in relation to a moving boat means a freer. A decelerating wind means a header.

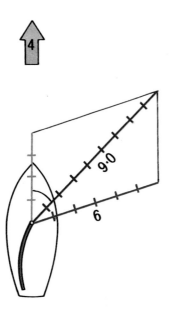 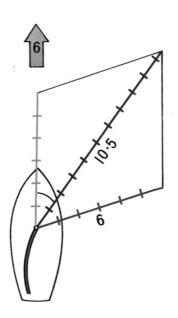 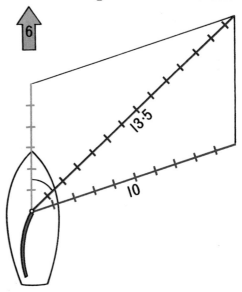

On the left, the 4 knots forward motion turns the 6 knot true wind (blue) into 9 knots apparent (red), and swings it forward. Increasing boat speed (centre) moves the apparent wind further forward and accelerates it to 10.5 knots. On the right the true wind has piped up to 10 knots, and the apparent wind has swung aft again.

In (B) the slower flow to windward of the foresail has headed the (dotted blue) wind to a new apparent direction (solid red). The mainsail therefore has to be sheeted closer to the centreline. In (C), faster flow to leeward of the main has the opposite freeing effect on wind approaching the headsail.

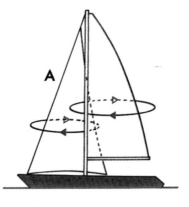

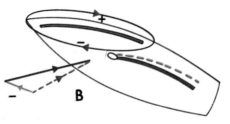

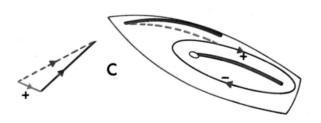

ing surface through the slot effect'. Both in fact contain an element of truth, but it is worth understanding what is actually happening.

The downwash from the jib is reducing the flow over the forward leeward surface of the mainsail. Slowing the flow has the effect of moving forward the apparent wind approaching the main, calling in turn for it to be sheeted closer to the centreline. Were it not, or equally the jib was sheeted in too tightly, this downwash effect from the jib would slow the flow between the two to the point where pressure equalised with that on the weather side of the mainsail and it would backwind.

A quite different story to the popular backwind theory of air building up, unable to escape through that all important narrow slot. In fact the whole slot theory of accelerated flow turns to dust when considered in these terms. Were the airflow through the slot between jib and mainsail indeed to be accelerated, then the jib would simply flop into the low pressure gap between the two.

By the same token, the jib, operating under the influence of the general circulation around the main, benefits from the subsequent upwash. This effectively increases and moves aft the apparent wind in which the foresail is operating. In other words, it gives the headsail a permanent lift.

The final step

Almost all that has gone before has been leading up to a clear understanding of this short section. How do the main and jib affect, and work together with, each other? It is also where a couple of widely held misconceptions are laid to rest

Both sails have their own general circulations, accelerating flow to leeward (upwash) and decelerating it to windward

(downwash). By placing them together as on a yacht, it becomes obvious that the mainsail is now working in the circulation around the jib, as is the jib in that of the mainsail (A).

The simple reasoning beloved of barside theorists goes something like: 'On a fractional rig, the jib acts as a guide bending the wind around to the lee of the driving mainsail. Or for the masthead rig, the small main acts like an aeroplane flap extending the lift-

25

This result is clearly seen from above, when to get both sails driving properly, the main has to be sheeted in at a narrower angle of attack than the forward sail. Were a mizzen included, then that would be sheeted even nearer to the centreline. As a matter of interest, although they had no helicopter from which to photograph the effect, square rig sailors knew all about this effect in practice. On a ship beating to windward, once each sail was sheeted to eliminate luff flutter, the angle of the yards could decrease by some 20 degrees between the forward and after mast.

The sum of the two parts then is to increase the effective power of the forward sail and diminish that of those behind it. Beating to windward the load per square foot on an efficiently trimmed jib, would be typically $1\frac{1}{2}$ times that on the main. The loads on a mizzen, were that rigged, would equate to $\frac{3}{4}$ per square foot of that of the mainsail.

Neither is all lost for those devotees of the need for a perfect slot. With the leech of the jib or genoa accurately aligned with the vertical camber of the mainsail lee, the slowing low pressure flow from the lee of the former can make the jump across to the lee of the main, re-energised by the latter's faster moving flow. When, and if, this happens, the total power producing flow over the lee of both sails becomes, in effect, as one, running from the foresail luff to the mainsail leech.

The relative angles of the yards on this ship can clearly be seen; with each square-sail sheeted in tighter than the one ahead.
Photo: Barry Pickthall

Sail cloth

The sailmaker, like any other engineer, has either to work within the properties of his raw material, or change them to better suit his needs. In the case of sailcloth the demands made by sailors, and particularly racing sailors, have recently accelerated the latter course.

That this acceleration has happened at the same time as an explosion in computer-aided information technology is no mere coincidence. Sail cloth manufacture, sailmaking and the needs of the recreational sailor account for a minuscule proportion of the industrial complex, with a corresponding dearth of funds for research and development. Yet the advent of the desk top computer is transforming sailmaking, from an art, firmly into a science. Even so, in the late eighties, there is not one sailmaker in the world who would claim to yet have all the answers.

The problem is, to say the least, complex. The aircraft designer, computing the best aerofoil for his wing, has the luxury of knowing it will not change shape once put to work. The sail designer knows that the first thing his aerofoil will do is to change its shape. The moment the sail fills into what is known as its flying shape, the forces, generated by the wind working against the restraining points where it is attached to the yacht, will distort what is basically a mobile membrane. The interaction of stresses does not end there. Were the wind to remain constant in speed and direction, the equation would be relatively simple, but it does not. Every small gust alters the equilibrium of the loads imparted, for example, by the sheet on the clew corner, as does every wave into which the yacht buries its bow.

A more detailed analysis of these structural stress problems more appropriately belongs in the section on shape design later, when the effect of wind on sails is discussed. Here it is merely introduced as an indication of why, over the past twenty years, the focus of attention has been on reducing the stretch in woven sailcloth, so closing the gap between the moulded shape, i.e. that which the sailmaker considers theoretically most efficient, and the flying shape once the sail is put to work.

If the impression so far is one that this search for better material has been motivated solely by the sail designer, then it is not wholly correct. While the large international sailmakers have developed and woven their own cloth to better meet the needs of their designers, the major sailcloth manufacturers have equally responded to the demands of their sailmaking customers and to competition from rivals. Bainbridge, for example, drawing on the needs of their worldwide customer base, maintain R & D facilities which far outstrip the resources of the smaller sailmakers, all of whom however directly benefit from each breakthrough achieved.

Computer terminals have displaced the drawing board in most lofts today. *Photo: North Sails Inc.*

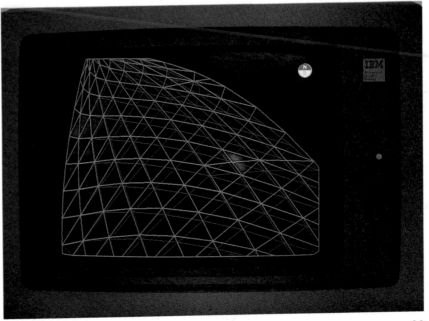

Photo: Bainbridge

Dacron

There are few sailors today with experience of any other material than polyethylene tetraphthalate for fore and aft sails. This is an oil-derived polyester, more popularly known as Dacron©; the trade name of the first commercial producers, E.I. du Pont de Nemours Inc. In countries outside America it is made by others with names that have entered each language. In Britain it is Terylene©; In France, Tergal©; Trevira© and Diolen© in Germany; Terlenka© in Holland; Terital© in Italy; and Teteron© in Japan. All are very similar, although there are some who maintain that, thanks to continued development, the original *Dacron* has managed to maintain a quality lead. Using the word *Dacron* from here onwards is purely for the sake of simplicity.

That this wonder material has until recently maintained a monopoly does nothing however to simplify the story. On the one hand, developments in weaving and finishing, hand in hand with superior sail construction techniques, could fill a book. On the other hand, because it is so ideal a raw material, many of the sails designed in its early days, using less developed weaves, are still flying today. For the sailor more interested in the sails he has, rather than those he might replace them with, it is worthwhile attempting to trace the development stage by stage. To do that it is necessary to understand the nature of woven material.

Dacron greige goods before finishing, ▲ magnified × 80. The warp (here horizontal) threads in this 6.5 oz. crosscut fabric have more crimp. Below, a single warp yarn, showing the crimp achieved during weaving.

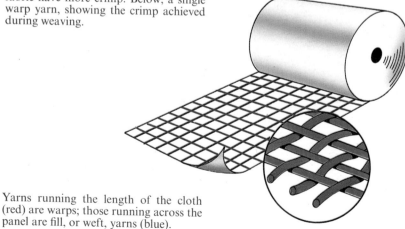

Yarns running the length of the cloth (red) are warps; those running across the panel are fill, or weft, yarns (blue).

30

The shuttle, carrying the fill yarn, can be seen emerging between the separated warp yarns on the left of this weaving loom.

Yarns

Dacron, in its emergent form is a filament. When twisted together, rather like a rope, they become a yarn. Even at this stage, in the search for less stretch in the finished product, there are a number of variables open to the designer, just as there are variable qualities of the filament itself. Early *Dacrons* for example, owed more to the needs of industrial and fashion users, than to the relatively tiny sailmaking market. Today's sailcloth designer has a say in the thickness of the filament and the number of twists per inch that each is given, both of which will affect the bulk and the strength of each yarn. At this, and virtually all other stages until the cloth is finished, the temperature and humidity during processing have to be very accurately controlled. Contrary to popular opinion *Dacron* absorbs water and this, in its formative life, can have a dramatic effect on the eventual tenacity of the yarn and therefore the cloth.

Interestingly, even the tension under which the yarn is wound onto its bobbin for delivery to the weaver is critical to its strength. All of these criteria add cost to the *Dacron* destined to be made into sails.

Warp and fill

In practice the sail cloth designer specifies two distinct types of yarn prior to their arrival at the weaving mill.

Cloth of all types is woven in lengths. In the case of some household textiles the run might extend to over 10 miles at a time. The width of the panel, on the other hand, is fairly constant, dictated by that of the loom—in the case of sailcloth, at this stage of its manufacture around 48 inches. The yarns specified to run the length of the cloth are called warp and those which will cross the panel, the weft or fill. For sailors, an easy way to remember the difference is to think of warps as the long 'ropes'.

During weaving the warps are stretched horizontally, side by side, through the loom. For each weave, frames pull the alternate warps vertically apart, and through the space between them, a bullet-shaped shuttle carrying the fill yarn shoots back and forth. Each fill strand is then slammed into place with great force. Because of the violence necessary to achieve the tight weave for sailcloth, much of this type of weaving is still done on looms whose appearance stems from a heavier industrial age, although newer high technology machines, modified for sail making, are coming into use in some parts of the world.

Quality control of the environment is still critical at this stage. A mill weaving *Dacron* for sailcloth would, for example, shut down automatically were the temperature and humidity to rise over 21 degrees C or 53 per cent respectively.

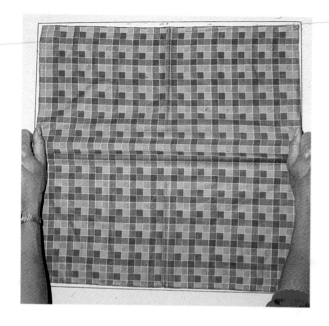
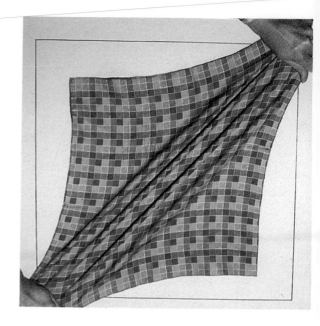

On the left, stretch along the yarn direction is minimal compared to that across the bias (right). Note how the sides and opposite corners have been drawn inside the original outline.

Bias

So far the strength either along or across the panel of cloth is fairly self-evident. It can be dictated by the cloth designer, by varying the tenacity of the warp, or fill yarns, either by varying their size or by increasing the number per square inch in one direction. This latter is known as the count. He can also control for example the relative stretch along the cloth panel by varying the degree with which the fill yarn distorts the warp yarn as it goes over and under it and vice versa. This is known as the 'crimp' factor.

At its most extreme the fill yarn across the panel would be absolutely straight, forcing the warp yarns to go over and under it. The stretch characteristics across the cloth would then be exactly the sum of the individual yarns. Along the length however, under tension, the warp yarns would try to straighten out, impossibly decreasing their tenacity. Obviously a balance has to be achieved in the amount of crimp of both the warp and the fill, particularly as their interrelationship has a direct bearing on the diagonal stretch across the cloth. This stretch across the bias is the sailmaker's real nightmare.

It is more easily shown with a looser weave cloth, such as used for a handkerchief. Pulled first side to side, the stretch depends on the resistance of the yarns (and their crimp which in this loose weave case is minimal). Now take hold of the diagonally opposite corners, and immediately the difference becomes apparent. What has happened is that the squares made by the criss-crossing warp and fill have now slipped into little diamonds with nothing to counteract the force directly on them other than the tightness of the weave.

The major developments since the early *Dacron* sails appeared in the mid-1950's have all been aimed at reducing this bias stretch, without compromising the important stretch resistance characteristics across the cloth

32

The same *Dacron* as earlier, but now after heat setting. The yarns have shrunk, and bulked out. The now permanant crimp locks the weave together.

panel. This fill orientation, as it is known, is the foundation upon which cross cut sails are built.

Heat setting

The adoption of *Dacron* for sails, and indeed its near 30 year monopoly, owes much to one property, which contributes above all others to its role as a sailcloth element. When heated the polyester yarns shrink and bulk up, and do so irreversibly.

Arriving at the finishing plant, the newly woven cloth, known at this stage as greige, is first cleaned to rid it of the lubricant (size) which is applied to the warp thread to assist weaving. In the early days the cloth would then be heated, either by passing through an oven or over heated rollers. Today the heating process is more gradual, and applied in stages concurrent with a whole range of other improvements and finishes. However in both cases the aim

would be the same, to expose it for a total of around a minute to a temperature of some 400 degrees Fahrenheit. The result of this injection of energy into the yarns is to build up a torque force between them, locking the weave to a point impossible to achieve mechanically on the loom.

This locking process, through heat, is irreversible, the cloth shrinking in the process along its length and across its width by around 20 per cent. The original greige cloth, some 48″ wide will, after heat treatment, be nearer 39″ across the panel.

The reduction in stretch across the bias achieved by this heat-induced, tightly packed weave is obvious. At its most simple this was the extent of the early *Dacron* sailcloth finishing process. Before expanding on how the process has been refined, it may be useful here to establish the basic problem that this work has sought to eliminate.

33

The concave 'collapse' between the three fixed corners is evident on the right.

The triangle shape

Again take the loosely woven handkerchief, but this time fold diagonally to represent a triangular sail shape, and pin down at head, tack and clew corners. By introducing, through a hole in the board underneath the triangle a force on its centre, broadly where the maximum differential in pressure would be on the real thing, two things become apparent.

The first is that all three of the unsupported edges cave in towards the point of force. In attempting to produce a triangular sail which will keep its shape, it is

this caving in along each edge which the sailmaker is striving to eliminate. For the sailor too, it is a fundamental lesson towards understanding how sails work.

Secondly, compare the degree of collapse towards the centre from the diagonal (luff), with that along the warp and fill edges. This is another simple illustration of the relative weakness of resistance to stretch across the bias compared with that along the direction of the warp and fill yarns.

Early Dacron

The first *Dacron* sails were in essence, very similar to their canvas predecessors. In fact one can trace the design elements directly back to the turn of the century.

Like so often today, it was the demands of the racing sailors which led to progress.

Ratsey and Lapthorn at Cowes are credited with the realisation that fill yarns across a panel were more stretch-resistant than their warp brethren. Until then, sails were scotch-cut, that is the panels were laid parallel to the leech of the sail, so that the weaker seams lay along the line of highest loading. By orientating the cloth panels at 90 degrees to the leech, and lining up the more stable fill yarns between head and clew, they achieved a breakthrough in leech control.

The introduction of *Dacron* did little to change the basic rules. With little or no say in how the

A sloop with scotch-cut sails. The panels, and warp yarns and seams, were all aligned with the loaded leech.

TURKS & CAICOS ISLANDS

E II R

BERMUDA SLOOP

10 c

Dacron was woven, the panel orientations continued as in the past.

For a mainsail, supported by spars along the luff and foot, the fill yarns were orientated parallel to the higher loaded leech. For the jib, with support only along the luff, the fill yarns were laid along both leech and foot. The panels met along a line which bisected the luff and clew angle called the mitre. This in itself caused a major problem as each panel met its partner in the other half of the sail on the bias, which naturally enough stretched and contracted more than the cloth around the edges. The skill with which the sailmaker cut his mitre-line to compensate was one of the main criteria upon which he was judged. In the mid-sixties, as the sail cloth designer began to exert an influence, the realisation grew that some control over the position of maximum camber within a sail could be made by harnessing the very bias stretch characteristics which until then had plagued them.

Prior to that time all headsails had a wire luff. By hardening it up, one achieved the depth of camber which the sail designer intended. If the wind increased or dropped, the sail was handed and replaced with a flatter or fuller sail as the case might be. There was absolutely no control over the po-

The panels in a mitre-cut sail were joined on the bias; calling for fine judgement by the sailmaker. *Photo: Colloryan.*

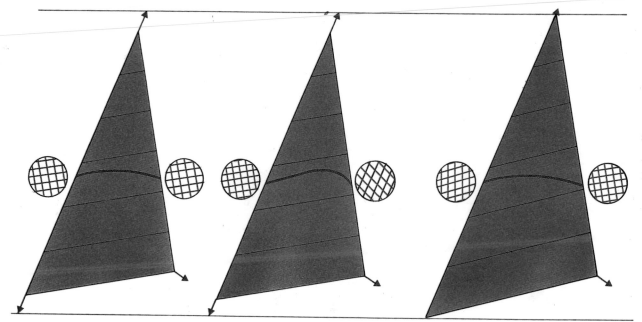

On the left, the fabric is balanced, but in the centre an increase in wind speed has pushed the camber aft, and stretched the square weave, near the leech, into diamonds. On the right, by stretching the luff, camber has been dragged forward again into the centre of the sail to re-balance it against the wind.

The panelling in the, now familiar, cross-cut headsail follows that of the better supported mainsail. *Photo: Alastair Black courtesy North Sails.* ▶

sition of the deepest point of draft, other than the questionable integrity of the cloth itself.

By discarding the wire luff rope, in favour of a heavy *Dacron* tape, it was realised that the tension between head and tack, that is along the luff, could be balanced against that of the sheet bisecting the clew. The bias factor throughout the sail, but particularly along the luff, could be harnessed to flatten the sail as the wind increased, and just as imortantly, to control precisely the point of maximum draft within the aerofoil section.

Whereas with the wire luff the flying sail shape had been a lottery between the forces working on the sail and those restraining it, now a third factor was introduced. With skill, and the necessary winch power available, the sailor could add to the equation by producing the desired shape in the conditions of the moment. One result was that fewer sails had to be carried, as each could be reshaped to cope with a wider band of wind speed. The other was the emergence on board the racing fleet of that exotic specialist: the sail trimmer.

Many sails still exist today which rely for their efficiency solely on this balancing act. The lack of inherent stability in the cloth itself dictates that the correct sail shape for any wind speed can only be achieved by balancing the tension between head and tack with that on the clew—in effect a full time, and as skilfully demanding as any, way to spend the weekend.

Filler

Meanwhile in the dinghy and smaller one-design fleets things were afoot, largely as a result of work by the sailcloth manufacturers. By introducing a filler material onto the woven cloth, they found they could reduce movement between the yarns, and therefore bias stretch, to the point that relatively low-stress headsails

for non-displacement boats could adopt the same cross-cut used for mainsails even though, unlike the mainsail, the headsail was supported along only one side. The advantages to the sailmaker in ditching the mitre-line were obvious. Again there were problems with the early fillers breaking down quickly leaving the cloth to fend for itself, and the fact that the coated cloths were distinctly stiff to handle and stow aboard a boat. The latter was so compelling an argument that one major sailmaker for many years successfully countered the claims of the evolving stiff cloths, by narrowing the

panel width of his uncoated 'soft' cloth in an effort to increase the user-friendliness of his product. At the time the tighter weave, narrow panel argument found much favour on the race course; but back in the laboratories another breakthrough was on the way.

Impregnation

The evolving chemistry of sail-cloth finishing accounted for the biggest strides forward, making *Dacron* a practical material for all cross-cut yacht sails. Breaking down a single heat setting process into a series of progressively hotter stages resulted in far greater

The Hood narrow-panel construction used a soft un-coated fabric with success.

control over the integrity of the finished product. A further refinement is impregnation. The cloth is immersed in a melamine solution which is chemically similar to the yarn. When heated, the *Dacron* yarns and melamine become as one. The molecules of both become aligned to form more durable and stretch-resistant fibres.

Unlike the early coatings, the impregnated melamine does not form a cement around each weave; neither does it affect the porosity of the cloth by filling the holes in between the fibres.

The relationship between warp and fill stretch remains the same as was designed into the weave in the first place. However, as stretch in each direction has been proportionally reduced, that across the bias is reduced even more, due to the stronger, tighter and more stable weave. Neither does the melamine add appreciable weight to the fabric. Indeed the additional strength imparted by the process allows the cloth de-signer to specify a lighter yarn in the first place.

Coating

Coating is a further refinement aimed at dramatically reducing stretch across the bias, in relation to that along and across the fabric. In the coating process the impregnated cloth is dipped through a bath of urethane 'glue' which is then forced into the weave as the cloth is squeezed past a heavy steel knife edge. When heat is applied the glue film hardens to cement the weave together. This is known as *yarn tempering*, a term originally proprietary to *Bainbridge*, but now part of the sailmaker's generic vocabulary. Its greatest effect is to lock the thread lines, drastically reducing bias stretch. The coating also fills the small gaps, or inter-cese, between the criss-crossing yarns, and gives a smooth finish to the cloth.

The resultant fabric epitomises the end of the road, as far as purely woven cloth is concerned, in the drive to eliminate the effect of wind strength distorting the flying shape of the sail. With elongation across the bias reduced almost to that along the fill, the sail designer can produce a sail that retains its shape without the need for constant balancing adjustment. On the other hand the very firm finish demands very careful handling. Equally the ex-

The same *Dacron* as earlier, but now with a *Yarn Tempered* finish. The 'soft' area round each interstice is the melamine coating.

The huge roller, to the right, gives an idea of the pressure exerted on the fabric during calendering.

cellent stability depends to an extent on the integrity of the coating which is less elastic than the *Dacron* base. Once stretched beyond its limit, the coating breaks down and the sail is virtually useless.

Calendering

With power dependent on the pressure differential on either side of the sail, porosity, or the degree by which air could seep from high to low pressure through the sail-cloth, counts for a great deal. The sailcloth finisher's main weapon against porosity is calendering, during which the fabric is passed between giant heated steel-rollers exerting literally tons of pressure to flatten the weave and seal the interstice between the interwoven yarns. Calendering also plays its part in tightening the weave further as it irons out and flattens each yarn. The resultant finish, smooth to the touch, adds to the cosmetic appeal of the cloth, but probably contributes little in pro-moting laminar or even turbulent power-producing flow over the finished sail.

So, from simple heat set *Dacron*, through impregnated and onto *yarn tempered* fabric, two distinct paths can be traced. The feel, or 'hand' of the cloth becomes both harder and stiffer as the ratio of bias to fill stretch is reduced. At its simplest, a resin free finish is soft on the hand, easy to stow, forgiving if subjected to stronger winds, but will need constant adjustment to produce a

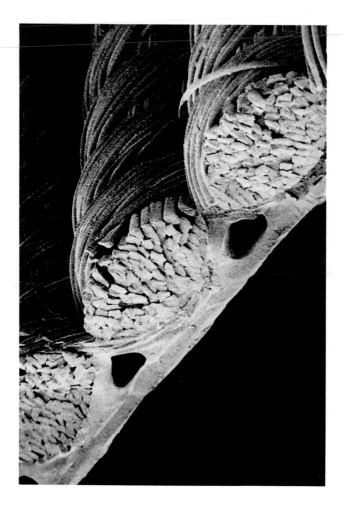

On the left, magnified × 80, a cross section through a *Kevlar/Dacron* laminate. The film, and glue, is under the woven substrate. On the right, the massive *Kevlar warps* for this vertical-cut laminate can be seen. The *Dacron* fill merely keeps them aligned.

fine flying shape. At the other end of the spectrum a *yarn tempered* fabric is stiff to handle, requires folding or even rolling to stow, will stretch irreversibly in excessive wind, but retains aloft the shape the designer intended. Even with tender loving care its life is measured in months compared to years for that of the resin free sail.

Between the two sits impregnated cloth in a multitude of grades of firmness and bias-to-fill ratios, each dependent on its weaving and finishing formula.

Mylar©

The ratio of stretch across the bias of a woven cloth therefore depends on (a) the tightness of the weave, and (b) the degree of finish. However tightly woven or highly finished the cloth is, the bias stretch will still be greater than along the primary direction of the yarns.

As far back as the late sixties, the sailmaker's frustration in at-

tempting to eliminate bias stretch led to experiments with a material, very similar chemically to *Dacron*, but physically yards apart. Whereas *Dacron* starts life as thin filament with molecules aligned in one direction, the new material, *Mylar*, is a film with the molecules orientated equally in all directions. The resistance to stretch of the *Mylar* is therefore the same both along and across the panel, and of course across the bias.

The first experimental *Mylar* sails were made simply by substituting film for woven cloth: but the drawbacks were soon apparent. The film was very easy to tear, particularly along the holes made by the sewing machines joining panel to panel. More importantly though to the sail designer, the equal stretch in all directions, characteristic of the film, generated more problems than it solved.

As will become apparent, in spite of the sailmaker's quest to reduce bias stretch, for a triangular sail to retain its shape against the forces acting upon it, a degree of bias stretch is essential. With pure film sails, for instance, there was simply no way that the draft position in a sail could be controlled.

Laminates

The answer lay in combining the advantages of both weave and film, by laminating the two together. Countless permutations of these have been experimented with, the major advantage being that the woven cloth, or substrate as it is known, can be dramatically lighter, for the same wind strength, than its all-woven counterpart. The major drawback on the other hand is in bonding the two materials together for anything like the same life-span as a conventionally woven fabric.

The many and varied attempts to solve the problems have dis-tilled into three broad answers. For very lightweight sails a loose woven scrim is sandwiched between two thin sheets of *Mylar*: for medium weight sails either a lightly woven *Dacron*, or from one manufacturer a knit-like scrim, is laminated to just one side of the film; and for heavyweight sails the film is laminated to one side of what is basically a tightly woven conventional sailcloth.

The space-lab environment surrounding this laminating machine gives a clue to the high cost of sails made from these materials. Adhesive coated substrate is emerging from the bridge-like heating tunnel and being mated with laminate from the roll in the foreground. *Photo: Hays Technology Systems/Dixon.*

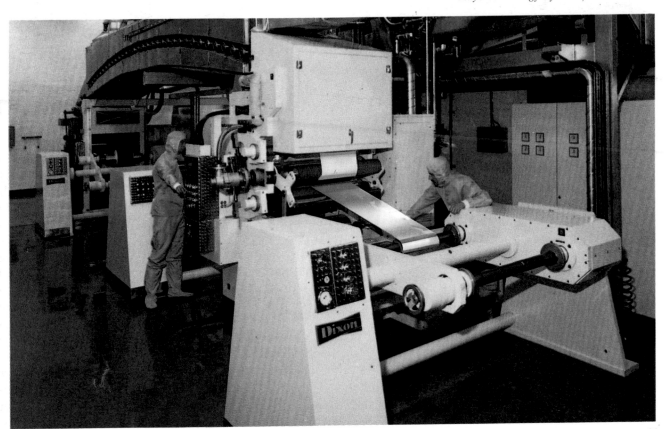

On the left, to the same scale as the earlier *Dacrons*, is the much more open weave of a *Dacron* substrate for *Bainbridge's Powerweave* laminate. On the right (at only 10 × magnification) is the open weave *Kevlar/Dacron* scrim of the same company's 3-ply laminate. The glue bonding laminate to laminate is glistening between the yarns.

In all cases the woven substrate can be designed with the same unbalanced characteristics as would be called for in conventional woven sails—the most obvious being a heavy fill orientation for laminate destined to be used in a cross cut heavily leech-loaded mainsail. Indeed, some of the exotic laminates in use on state of the art racing yachts incorporate yarns other than *Dacron* within the substrate to reinforce the laminate in one direction. *Kevlar©* is one of these yarn fibres used in areas of very high loading. *Spectra©* is another.

The techniques of laminating *Mylar* to its substrates are closely guarded secrets. This reluctance on the part of the cloth manufacturers stems largely from their individual efforts in reducing the tendency for the film to delaminate from the substrate.

Early laminates also suffered from stiffness due to the glue used to make the bond. Much of the development of softer and long lasting *Mylar* laminates can be laid at the door of better thermoset glues which achieve a strong and flexible chemical bond through both heat and pressure—the actual manufacturing process being akin to that used to produce veneer-type laminates for the furniture industry.

Whatever the secret formulae involved in their production might be, laminates are seen by many as the sailcloth of the future, and not only for the racing sailor. By relying on the film to contain bias stretch the manufacturer can concentrate on designing less compromising, and far lighter sail cloth to meet the sailmaker's specific needs.

The story of how each development has played its role in the shaping of the sails now belongs to the sailmaker.

The increasingly familiar dark yellow panels of *Kevlar* laminate, reinforcing the leeches of both fore and mainsail.

Sailmaking

The sailmaker's task is to take flat woven cloth and turn it into a three dimensional shape which is aerodynamically efficient. It is a task which is easier to define than to execute.

First a short recap of the problems raised so far, along with the establishment of fundamental goals to be achieved.

Fabric distorts under load, and the loadings, or stresses, on a sail at work are continually changing. Even if the sailmaker could produce a perfect moulded shape, once set under load it would distort. From the outset, stretching right back to the specification of the basic yarn, each element is geared to producing the flying shape.

Time therefore to consider that three dimensional shape.

Two appear obvious. Every sail has height and length, in other words the dimension of its plan form. The third dimension is the depth of the sail, or camber. It is this of course that generates lift, and, as has been explained, a very large proportion of drag. The depth of a sail is measured at any point up and down the sail—and it varies from head to foot—as a ratio between the horizontal distance across the sail, known as a chord, and the deepest point of camber. This depth-to-chord ratio, usually expressed as a percentage, is one measurement the sail designer uses to specify the aerodynamic shape at varying heights of the triangle. The other is the point of deepest camber along the chord, known as the maximum depth location.

A full size genoa therefore might have a 17 per cent depth-to-chord ratio one third down from the head, compared with only 15 per cent for the flatter mainsail working in its downwash. A smaller heavy-air genoa could be as low as 14 per cent at the same height. The maximum depth location for all should not be more than 50 per cent aft, and as will be seen when foresails are discussed in detail later, in strong winds and rougher seas, considerably further forward.

Twist

Once the sail is filled with wind, its chords will not remain in the same plane. Those further from the point of restraint, i.e. the sheet, will under load, progressively twist off to leeward. There is more than one school of thought about why twist is necessary; this will be touched on in the description of mainsails. That it has to be calculated into the design is agreed upon however, if only to ensure that when the luff of the sail is correct, the wind flow can exit from the leech in the most efficient manner. The designed twist in a sail is specified by progressively increasing towards its head the angle between chords and the centre line of the boat.

The horizontal, or chord measurement (A), and the point of maximum depth (B).

Photo: Rick Tomlinson/PPL

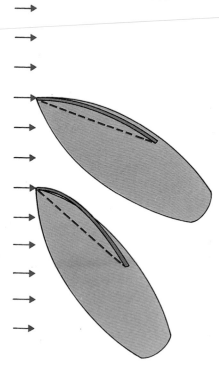

A fine leading edge angle (top) allows the boat to point higher. In rougher water however, the coarser leading edge (below) will delay the sail stalling.

Leading edge angle

Both the depth-to-chord ratio and the maximum depth location have a bearing on the degree of camber at the all-important leading edge of the sail. It is here, particularly in the case of a foresail, less so for the main shadowed by a mast, that aerodynamic power for the whole sail is shaped.

A flat or fine entry will allow the boat to point higher into the apparent wind, but because the maximum draft is proportionally further aft the drag increases, as does the chance of stalling flow over the leeward surface. A flat entry is not forgiving.

A round entry on the other hand, whilst not allowing one to

46

point high, means that maximum camber is forward, increasing lift and reducing drag with a flatter leech section. Because the sail is less likely to stall, helming does not have to be so precise. Full or round entry sails come into their own in higher winds and rougher seas when it is impossible to point precisely.

Here one begins to see the need for some bias stretch to allow for depth position adjustment on all sails, even those made from the most structured materials. In the past such niceties depended solely on the skill and commitment of the sailor coaxing shape into unstable cloth. Today, materials call for the designer to take much more account of building such refinements into the sail from the start.

Design today

To see how the sail designer squares up to the geometrical complexities of producing an efficient flying shape, it is worth breaking down the problem into its constituent parts. On the one hand he has the aerodynamics of what makes the most efficient shape, and on the other the structural limitations of the material from which he has to produce that shape.

The fundamental problem is that these two are dependent on each other. It is rather like a soap bubble which exists only by an equilibrium of surface tension and the difference in pressure inside and out. The sail's shape is similarly an equilibrium of pressure versus surface tension and in theory could be resolved math-

ematically by application of what is known as a membrane equation. As load is put on the sail, it changes the stresses therein, which changes the shape, which changes the pressure, or load again, and so on. Solving this cause and effect cycle would depend on knowing what pressures are developed on the sail aerodynamically, and what stresses it is subject to, both within and at the edges. Unfortunately the answers to neither are complete.

Some of the aerodynamic answers have been found, mainly from basic lifting surface techniques used in the aircraft industry in the late 1960s, as have some of the stress load factors using finite element methods and load gauges. What is known has brought the sailmaker in the past dozen or so years from that of being a craftsman to a devoted manipulator of the desk-top computer.

Even so, design still owes as much to empirical experience gleaned whilst on the water, as to mathematical theory. Computers as the supposed parents of the perfect sail are a widespread marketing tool, but their limitations in that role were highlighted in an all-too-rare glimpse into sail development at the leading edge, by winning America's Cup skipper John Bertrand in his enthralling

In the 1987 America's Cup, the *Kookaburras* fitted micro-video cameras inside their masts, feeding pictures directly into a computer, which could evaluate sails. The broad camber stripes enabled the cameras to 'read' the sail's shape. *Photo: Nick Rains/PPL*

money being of very little object, the empirical approach was relied upon. Just as does any loft with an interest in fast sails, listening to what its own staff and recognised quick sailors say about each sail when they come off the water.

With hand on heart, however, there is not a sailmaker in the world today who will admit to saying 'for this boat, in the wind speed, in these wave conditions, this is the best sail shape—and the way we will produce it is such and such.' What the large international lofts can say—mainly because of their greater resources and research and development programmes—is 'we can use mathematical methods and computers to produce consistent sail shapes. That consistency allows us to build a data base with which to develop a theoretically better shape on the water'.

If this sounds like a plug for the large lofts, it is not necessarily so. The benefits of smaller, friendlier, local and less technological sailmakers are well recognised, as is their ability, particularly for boats they know well, to often produce faster sails than those by the big names. It is a fact however, in an increasingly scientific arena, that R & D is the way forward.

Stress mapping

Empirical methods can also throw light on the stresses to which a sail is subjected, particularly those within the plane of

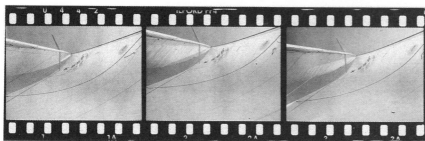

account of the 1983 series 'Born to Win'.

Throughout their campaign, and every day they sailed off Newport, the Australians photographed their sails, cross referencing each shot with a computer print-out of boat and wind speed plus a measure of sailor's seat-of-the-pants. Each evening the

pictures were poured over to see what shape was fast, and each night the sails were recut to reproduce the fastest shape in the photographs.

Of course, the details were added to the computer data base for future new sails but this was a classic example of how, with theory, computers, and indeed

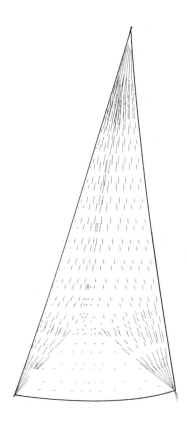

A typical stress map of a high-aspect ratio foresail. Each red line, or cross, represents the degree, and direction, of stress for warp and/or fill. *Courtesy Sobstad.*

Computer programmes allow any sail shape to be viewed from any angle—invaluable when designing in all the variables. *Courtesy: Island Computer Systems, Cowes.*

the sail. Load gauges attached to clew and tack not only register the stress at these points but when co-ordinated with photographs of the whole sail can point the way to understanding the loads within. The aim is to understand and put computer-digestible numerical values to what was happening in the simple triangular handker-chief demonstration earlier.

It has been perfectly obvious for years that the greatest loading on a mainsail, for example, is be-tween head and clew. Try pushing the leech of a sheeted-in mainsail, and then do the same thing to the luff. There is no comparison be-tween the tensions in each.

That in itself is of course not enough. The thrust of research is to find the comparative stresses on each and every point through-out the sail, from its area of high-est loading, to that of its lowest—the place, somewhere near the middle of the triangle where, if

one made a hole, it would form a perfect circle, undistorted by stresses from any of the attach-ment points.

For every set of luff, leech and foot lengths the stress map will be different, and again, the map for a high aspect mainsail will differ in detail from that for a generally much lower aspect, full size genoa. Basically however the lines of isostatic stress are similar. They collapse inwards from each edge of the triangle towards the centre.

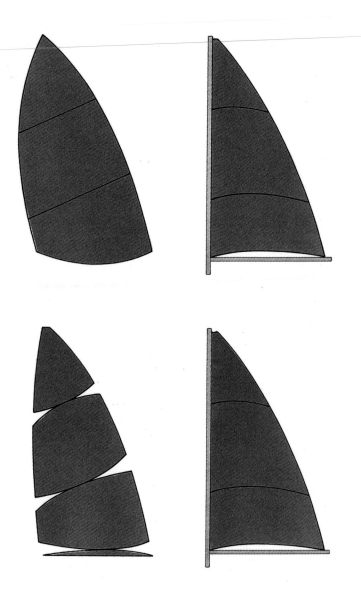

Top left, a large luff roach, or curve, when set on a straight mast (top right) will give camber to the sail. As will tapered seams and a less acute luff curve (below).

Catenaries

These curved lines between the attachment corners of highest stress are known as catenaries. The principle has long been recognised in the hollow, or concave curve given to the foresail leech. Were the leech cut in a straight

line between head and clew, tensioning it would simply produce a harder and straighter leech edge with no effect on the adjacent area, in effect hooking it to windward. By hollowing the curve between top and bottom, the leech edge under tension straightens out aftwards, dragging the adjacent cloth with it and flattening the whole area.

Exactly the same applies to the mainsail except that battens

allow this hollow to be extended outwards into a convex roach curve, about which more later. Battenless mainsails have to have a hollow leech.

Jibs and genoas can be cut with either a hollow or, for the latter, a roach along the foot, while mainsails almost always have foot roach added.

Luff curve

The final dimension the sailmaker has to consider when formulating his sail shape is the degree of curve given to the luff.

In the days of less stable cloths, including early *Dacrons*, the camber in each sail was introduced by adding a convex curve to the luff. When set on a straight forestay or mast, this extra cloth fell back into the sail, providing the camber between luff and leech. In effect the camber depended for its fairness on the equilibrium between wind and the integrity of the cloth. This in itself was not much of a bargain, particularly as excess cloth from the luff curve was basically in the forward part of the sail.

With the advent of more stable, structured cloths came what is generically known today as broadseaming. The camber is built into the sail by tapering the edges of a number of cross-cut panels, so that when they are sewn together, camber is locked in. This technique has drastically reduced the amount of luff curve necessary. The afore-mentioned foot roach achieves the same result along the lower edge of the mainsail. When set on a straight boom, the excess cloth is pushed into the lower sail, forming a shelf.

When calculating the luff curve for a foresail, the sail designer has a further complication. Under load, sag in the forestay will allow cloth to move back into the body of the sail increasing the degree of camber. To counteract this he must reduce the amount of convex luff, and even in some circumstances replace it with a concave shape.

Sail cloth

These then are the numerical factors the sail designer must define before even a moulded shape is possible. Remembering at this point that, with the exception of class boats where the dimension of sails is strictly controlled, the basic dimensions of those for most yachts will differ.

Equally, into the equation, the better sailmaker must take account of how the customer's boat will be sailed; is it a pure cruiser, round-the-world racer, a 12 Metre, or something in between? To say nothing of the depth of that same customer's pocket.

It is with these choices in mind that the final ingredient is shaken into the design cocktail.

Fabric specification

Already in the computer— and we can begin to see why sailmakers have taken to them like ducks to water—is a numerically

Computerised stretch and recovery testing produces the result directly onto a graph. The sail sample is being stretched between the two white box-like jaws in the foreground.

A typical *Dacron* stretch graph. The black lines represent a virgin fabric sample under load. The red are for similar fabric, but after being fluttered. The lower pair show elongation in the fill direction, and the upper pair, that on the bias. Horizontal scale shows tension loadings in pounds. The vertical scale represents 100 units for elongation percentages.

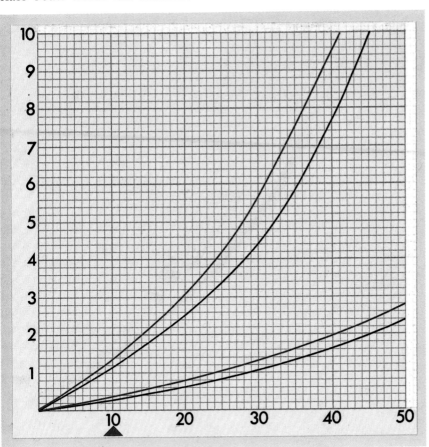

moulded shape. To transform it into anything like a suitable flying shape, the characteristics of the cloth have to be added.

Enough has been written previously to show how cloth characteristics can be varied by design. Less obvious maybe is the unfortunate fact that cloths of identical specification can end up, through variables in the manufacturing process, with quite different stretch characteristics. If the sailmaker's aim is development based on consistency of a given

51

Working to an outline on the loft floor, the sail area is filled with fabric.

point is reached across the fill when the cloth yields and the line on the graph moves sharply skywards. This is the point above which the cloth will not recover—in effect its upper wind limit.

Interestingly, the 16″ × 2″ cloth sample size originates, the story goes, from Lowell North who, dissatisfied with cloth variations set in train a series of tests. One of these, designed to flutter cloth before stressing it, was to tie a strip of cloth to his car aerial before driving home each evening. The round trip, back again next morning took 30 minutes and the strip, yes, was 16″ × 2″. Flutter tests today are, if less romantic, somewhat more controlled.

Offsets

The result of all of these mathematical variables, once fed into and crunched by the computer, is a list of numerical lengths across various stations in the triangle, from which a flat shape can be drawn on the sail loft floor.

Known as offsets, these will include the luff and foot lengths, and in the case of a foresail, a perpendicular length from a point on the luff to the clew. There will also be a number of lengths at specific stations up and down the triangle describing the necessary curves for the luff and leech. In the case of a mainsail these will also allow for the curve of the roach.

A fair curve is then outlined around these offset points as a guide, at this stage, for the cutter

series of moulded shapes, he must know precisely the characteristics of each piece of cloth he uses.

The answer lies in a series of tests to which each batch of sail cloth is subjected. Of course, as well as revealing the comparative qualities of the particular batch, the tests also establish, in the first place, the suitability of that particular weave, finish and weight for a particular sail. In practice these criteria would be fed into the sail design process at a very early stage. Indeed in some cases they would be the starting point, and the very reason for, a particular design development. The graphs resulting from a batch test will be

merely fulfilling a fine tuning role, and there are those in the sail cloth making business who decry some sailmakers' reluctance to make the most of them.

The basic test is one for stretch and recovery. A sample strip 16″ long and 2″ wide is pulled between two jaws at a slow but steady rate. Progress of the rate of stretch across the fill and along the bias is plotted on a graph. As can be seen on page 51, at ten pounds this medium finish 4.4 oz cloth has a 0.03 inch stretch on the fill, and 0.12 inch on the bias. It becomes known as a 3 to 12 cloth. A *yarn tempered* cloth might be as low as 2 to 4. As the load increases a to allow enough cloth to make the sail with minimum wastage.

First layout

In recent years a number of exotic panel layouts have emerged in the search for more stable sail shapes, but still ninety-five per cent of main and foresails remain cross-cut, that is with the fill yarns aligned along the direction of the high loaded leech.

Working perpendicularly to a line between head and clew, the cloth is rolled panel by panel until the entire outline on the loft floor is filled.

The final process in finishing the cloth before delivery to the sailmaker is to seal the edges either by heat or laser, and to scribe a selvage line inboard from each edge. This allows the sailmaker to line up each panel with an accurate overlap for eventual seaming. Pencil marks are made across adjacent panels on the floor so that each may be aligned accurately during the next stage when they are joined together.

Panel plans

Whilst the computer has a role in the design of sails for smaller class boats, the dimensions of many are strictly controlled by their governing association. Equally many are of a size for which patterns can be stored. It is true also to say that the empirical approach to the shape within the limited plan form dimensions of a class keel-boat sail is far more productive, as like can be compared to like on the water.

Consequently sailmakers keep full size patterns for the panels of many of these types of sails; updating curves and cuts as a direct result of how well each sail performs on the race course.

In place of the lofting layout as previously described, the panels are cut using a template which reflects the state of the particular sailmaker's knowledge of that class. It is not unusual for a performance sailmaker to have six different patterns for one class mainsail, all related to such variables as wind range and types of sea conditions in which the boat will be sailed. Such panels will of course already incorporate the curves necessary to provide, when sewn together, the camber in the sail.

For smaller keelboat sails, panel plans are maintained with constant updates from the race course.

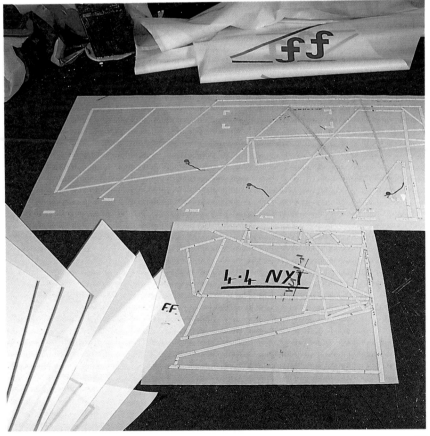

Broadseaming. Above left, the panel taper is outlined with double-sided sticky tape. Above right, the excess cloth is removed; and below right, the two adjacent panels are joined ready for stitching.

Broadseaming

Returning to the sail laid out on the loft floor, early, unstructured *Dacron* panels would have gone straight from there to a machinist to be sewn together. Each seam was straight, the sail depending on its eventual camber, on excess cloth in the luff curve. With today's cloth that shape is built in by tapering the overlapping seams of a number of the panels towards the luff and leech. This is broadseaming, and is done by hand to very precise amounts laid out in the original offsets.

Double-sided sticky tape is

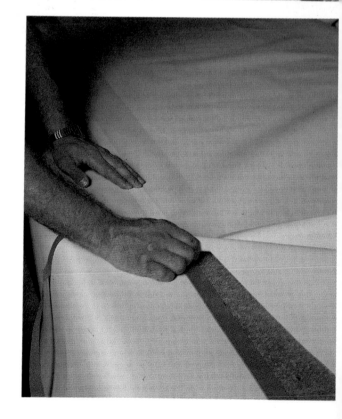

first accurately laid along the points originally marked during layout of those seams to be shaped. Each is then cut to that outline. Whether broadseamed or not, panel is now joined to panel, using double-sided sticky-tape, before being passed on for sewing.

In the case of a laminate sail, a much stronger double-sided adhesive *Dacron* tape would be used to join each panel. This overcomes one of the early problems with *Mylar* sails, where the stitching along each seam had a tendency to creep when the sails came under load. Inserting a woven tape between the Mylar films provides enough substance to counteract this creeping.

Computerised cutting

In the process described so far, the role of the computer is nothing more than an aid to design. The sailmaking process itself is little changed from that in the days of Nelson. Cloth panels are laid out and cut to fit a shape drawn on the loft floor, and will shortly be sewn together.

However, the future is already here. A future in which the design goes directly from the computer via a floppy disc onto an automatic cutting table which shapes each panel automatically. How quickly this computer-aided manufacture will take over is another question. The machines, incorporating such exotica as laser cutters are extremely expensive, and will probably remain, for some time, the preserve of the large international lofts. Certainly in the latter half of the 1980s, just as in Nelson's day, there are 12 Metre sails of extraordinary cut and complexity being fashioned panel by panel on the loft floor.

Seaming

Returning to the conventional loft, the sail, with panels joined with sticky tape, is now ready to be sewn together.

Equating the sheer bulk of material with the need for accurate seaming has led sailmakers to devise numerous layouts for their seaming operations, from

New computer cutters work straight from the designers' floppy disk, automatically cutting each panel with either a fast spinning knife, or a laser beam. *Photo: North Sails Inc.* ▼

This machinist at Hood's British loft is sewing panels for a 65 foot yacht's headsail. ▼

Each chevron in the upper 3 rows is made from six individual stitches. The lower rows are more familiar.

the simple table-top for small sails, to holes in the loft floor in which the machinists sit. Efficiency is the name of the game; particularly when one considers that each seam may have to pass through the sewing-machine three or four times.

One of the methods used to reduce stretch along the heavily loaded leech for example is to add an extra thickness of cloth to each panel between the head and clew. This two-ply layer would have been cut on the floor along with the other panels. A typical seaming schedule for such a mainsail for a 35 foot boat would call for four rows of stitches through the two ply areas, reducing to three in the middle of the sail and two as

The luff is cut with a fair curve.

56

the seam nears the luff. These rows would be of the narrow zig-zag type with which all sailors are familiar.

A new development on large sails is for each zig-zag to be made up of three individual stitches. This reduces the size of the seam, making the sail more flexible and easier to handle, and may reduce skin friction. One large seam is also quicker, and therefore cheaper to sew; but the cost of the machines is high.

The thread used is of a contrasting colour. This apparently minor point fulfils two important functions.

It allows the sailmaker, and later the sailor, to see if any threads are frayed or broken; vital as *Dacron* or laminate sails are so unyielding. The stitching will always remain proud and therefore exposed to chafe. Secondly, a contrasting colour along each seam allows the sailor to read the camber shape once the sail is up and drawing.

Second layout

The seamed sail is now returned to the loft floor for the final shaping of the three sides. The most important of these is the luff, the curve of which plays such an important role in the eventual three dimensional shape.

In some cases the original computer offset points for the luff curve will already have been marked on the appropriate panels. If not, they will be measured and marked now, as will those along the leech and foot. Sailmakers' prickers will then be stuck through the cloth into the loft floor. Around these, long flexible battens are bent to give a fair curve before the excess cloth is trimmed off.

Reinforcing patches are added to each corner.

It is usual at this stage to add reinforcing patches and, if necessary for large sails, stress tapes, to take the extra high loadings in the three corners.

On a conventional cross-cut *Dacron* sail these are simply triangular shaped layers of cloth progressively reducing in depth, but on some of the more exotic cuts and materials, they may be complicated radial lay-ups and even unidirectional laminates. A glance at the stress map reveals the concentration of load in these

58

areas which reinforcing has to counteract without distorting the rest of the sail.

Stretching

Most sails made today depend on their flying shape to some degree on adjustable tension along the luff and, in the case of the mainsail, also along the foot. However they are attached to the rig, whether it is by hanks, sliders or the modern equivalent of a bolt-rope, they feature some sort of heavy and adjustable tape along the luff of both headsails

and mainsails, and along the foot of the latter. The degree of control along these edges is dictated by the stretch resistance of the heavier, and stronger, material.

Along the leech of both, and along the foot in the case of the headsail, a hem or tabling has to be added to stop the cloth from fraying. These added thicknesses of cloth reduce the stretch around the edges of the sail compared to that in its body. Under tension the leech would become hard and hooked.

This large headsail for a 60 foot yacht, being stretched out at Hood's loft, costs more than a family car.

◀

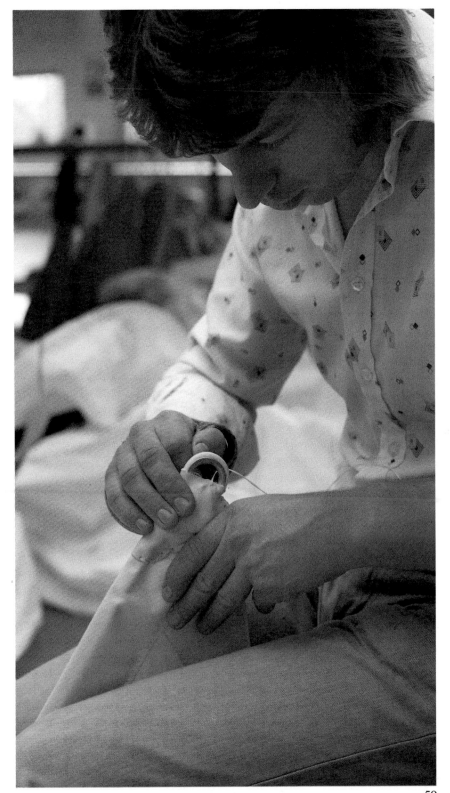

To counteract this, the sail is stretched before the tapes and tabling are attached to them. It is stretched out between three strong points in the loft and the tapes and tabling married to the edges, usually with staples to keep them in place until final finishing and stretching.

It is under the folded tabling that lines are run for controlling the leech of both headsails and mainsails.

Finishing

The final stage covers a multitude of techniques or skills, from swaging in steel cringles with heavy hydraulic presses, to hand sewing leather chafing pads around the clew corners. Sailmakers pride themselves on their finishing details, many of which find their way into their advertisements. It is somehow accepted that the basic sail will work and that what makes one product better than another is the addition of some small marketing trim.

On the other hand, many of these ancillaries make a definite contribution to both the efficient use and consequent enjoyment of sails today. Some of these will become apparent as each sail is examined in more detail.

Hand finishing a cringle with soft leather patching is a highly skilled job. ▶

The mainsail

In practice the mainsail must perform a number of roles, each of which provides an insight into the three-dimensional shape with which every sailor is familiar. It is worthwhile, before looking in detail at this all-purpose sail, to set out the demands made upon it.

It will be remembered from an earlier chapter that when beating to windward both main and foresail should work as one, the former optimising the circular flow effect around the latter, and vice versa. Whilst the foresail—or the forward part of the rig—develops the greater proportion of power, it can only achieve that thanks to the upwash provided courtesy of the main.

The mainsail shape has also to be married to that of the foresail, forming one power-producing curve.

Staying with that thought, the mainsail leech has now become the trailing edge of the rig. In addition to extending the power-producing curve, it must also provide an efficient trailing edge shape to reduce as far as is possible the effects of those induced-drag trailing buckets.

The relationship of this trailing edge to the centreline of the boat has a significant effect on the helm, rather like that of flaps on an aircraft. If sheeted too far to windward, lift moves aft upsetting the balance between rig and keel which has to be counterbalanced with the rudder, i.e. weather helm.

The main is also an all-purpose sail. As the wind increases so the mainsail must be capable of being first flattened, and then reduced in area, whilst still fulfilling its partnership with the foresail.

With the wind free, on a reach, and with the influence of the foresail diminished, the main must still be capable of producing a high degree of lift in the direction of travel.

Finally, running before the wind it must be capable of reversing everything that has gone before. Ignoring spinnakers for the moment, it now becomes the primary sail which must generate maximum drag from the following wind.

How then are these criteria met, and what effects have they had on the development of today's modern mainsail?

First and foremost, there must be an overriding facility for adjustment to meet these roles. This applies to the camber, or cross section of the sail as much as it does to the plan form.

Support in tension

Unlike the foresail, our main has support along two of its sides—the mast supports the luff and the boom the foot. Whilst it is true that the sail is primarily held between the head, tack and clew points, the support provided by the spars along luff and foot plays a significant role.

Consider the stress map of a typical mainsail. Once filled with wind all three sides of the triangle naturally want to cave in, or collapse, towards the centre. The sides attached by slides, or a bolt-rope, to mast and boom are restrained. The leech on the other hand, relies only on tension between the halyard at its head and the sheet, and to a lesser extent, the boom-outhaul at its clew, for support. Of course, because the other two sides are unable to collapse, the desire on the part of the leech is also that much stronger; so much so, that virtually the total shape of a mainsail on the wind is dictated by the loading between the head and clew of the sail. Unless the catenary between these two points can be straightened there is little hope of controlling the depth of camber in the body of the sail.

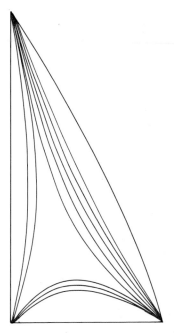

The red catenary lines show the stress paths within the sail.

Photo Rick Tomlinson/PPL

A *Dacron* weave for a high-aspect cross cut mainsail magnified × 80. The thick uncrimped fill yarns run top left to bottom right.

Hence the sailmaker's preoccupation to reduce stretch in the highly loaded leech. Since the early 1900s the route taken has been to align the fill yarns, over which much greater control can be achieved during weaving along this line of loading.

Leech control

As cloth weaving and finishing techniques have developed, so *Dacrons* designed solely for this job have emerged, each with stronger straighter fill yarns relative to those along the warp. These fill-orientated weaves have in turn led to higher aspect ratio mainsails, where the height of the sail relative to its length between tack and clew has increased. The modern IOR masthead main epitomises this trend, as does the even more recent ultra-high aspect ratio heavy-weather blade jib.

Typically a cloth used in a high aspect main would have a fill bias ratio of maybe 2 to 16, compared to that of around 2.5 to 9 for a genoa.

That is only the beginning of the story for high performance mainsail leech constructions. As noted earlier, two-ply mainsails

The saw-edge on this two-ply leech helps blend the high loads into the less resistant single ply forward area.

are very common today even on pure cruising boats. By using a lighter-weight cloth throughout the sail, but adding an extra layer along the loaded leech, strength is retained where needed, and the overall weight aloft is reduced.

The advent of very low stretch exotic laminates incorporating *Kevlar*, an aramid fibre, has extended this leech reinforcing theme in a multitude of geometric configurations familiar to anyone watching top class racing boats in action. The most sophisticated are no longer content to align the strength directly between head and clew, but follow a complicated layout with panels orientated along the catenary lines of the leech.

One of the benefits following in the wake of laminate development, is the ability it gives the designer to unbalance the material in either fill or warp direction. By orientating stronger and stronger warp yarns within the substrate, thoughts can revert to the original scotch, or vertical, cuts of old. These it will be recalled were favoured because they allowed the weaker seams to be orientated along, rather than across, the high leech loadings.

Here the *Kevlar* panels closely follow the catenary route between head and clew. Note the intricate reinforcing panel structure dissipating the high loads at the head of this Banks' mainsail.

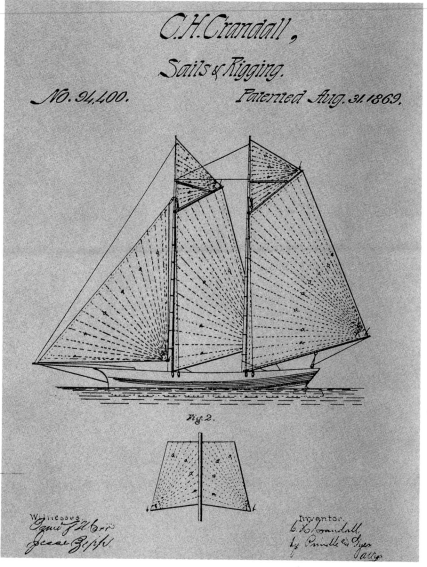

Fig. 2.

▲ A problem with radial contructions is that the triangular panels have to be cut across, or off, the parallel threadlines (A). *Bainbridge* have developed a sophisticated weave, in which the dominant warp yarns actually radiate out along each panel (B).

◄

The first radial cut suit of sails?

Aramid yarns, such as *Kevlar*, are incorporated with the substrate to reinforce these laminates. *Kevlar* is responsible for the dark yellow panelling in some constructions. Weight for weight it is three or four times as stretch resistant as *Dacron*, but is prone to work-harden from constant bending or flexing. *Spectra*, a polyethylene fibre, is the latest reinforcement. Said to be ten times the strength of steel, *Spectra* is also less prone to abrasion and flex fatigue.

These then are the elements behind the re-emergence of a vertical cut for high performance sails. The drawback is that the broadseaming necessary to build a fair shape into the sail is much more complicated to resolve vertically, across the flow, than it is horizontally. Spherical geometry of this magnitude makes even computers go hot.

Another avenue is to line up heavily warp orientated laminates along the stress lines radiating into the sail from one or more of its three corners. These radial cuts, at first glance, follow a theme developed in the production of spinnakers. Few ideas in the world are new however. A search through the patent files of, in this case, America, shows that someone else had the same thought more than 100 years ago.

All constructions, from the modest to ultra sophisticated, have the same aim. To reduce stretch along the leech, the one area in the mainsail where it is not wanted.

Bias

Conversely, because of the need to be able to adjust the mainsail over a wide range of shapes, some stretch in other areas is beneficial. With the fill yarns aligned along the leech, panelling in the body, and particularly at the luff and foot, is angled such that loads are across the bias.

Whilst much of the development work with *Dacron*, and latterly the laminates, has been directed at reducing bias stretch, a degree has to be retained, particularly in the mainsail. For it is upon this bias that much of the adjustment in the camber of the mainsail depends.

For windward work it is essential for the main to provide a flat sectioned leech from which the airflow over both sails can exit. Equally, before that flow even reaches the leech, it is essential that the vertical camber in the body of the main can be married to that of the foresail leech.

The slot

The faster, low pressure flow generated over the lee surface of the headsail is slowing down and increasingly prone to misbehave as it nears the leech. The aim must therefore be to re-energise the flow and by so doing, delay separation until the leeward flow reaches the leech of the mainsail.

The re-energising force comes from the relatively fast flow exiting off the lee of the main through the gap between the two, known to all as the slot. As this exits it attracts and speeds up again the flow over the lee of headsail.

For any rig and windspeed there is an optimum width of slot which equally should be as close as possible to vertically constant. Too wide and the accelerating low pressure flow on the lee of the main will not be close enough to

that coming off the lee of the foresail to attract and extend its journey. Too narrow and the slow moving high pressure to windward of the headsail will brake the velocity of the flow across the lee of the main. When this happens to the point that flow and pressure on both sides of the mainsail luff equate, it backwinds. Thereafter the ability of the flow over the lee of the main to accelerate again in time to attract that from the lee of the headsail is severely hampered. Either way the lift producing flow across the two sails is partly, or wholly, broken—wholly if the total slot is either too wide or too narrow; partly if the width of the slot between the two sails is not constant. It is essential therefore to be able to match camber in the body of the mainsail to the shape of the headsail leech.

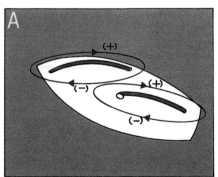

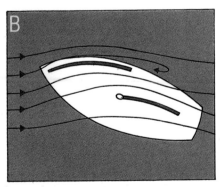

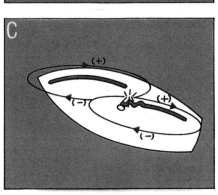

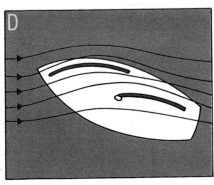

The slot contributes to effective circular flow (A). Too wide (B) and flow from the headsail lee will separate; too narrow (C) and the circular flows collide. In (D) the two sails work together at their optimum.

Camber, as was seen earlier, is designed into a sail in one of two ways. In earlier unstructured *Dacrons* a convex curve of additional cloth was added to the luff. Once set on the straight mast this cloth was pushed back into the sail giving it its third dimension. However, due to the high bias stretch inherent in such *Dacrons*, as the wind increases, so the position of maximum camber is blown aft and similarly the depth-to-chord ratio increases. A counterbalance in force is necessary to preserve the equilibrium.

This is where the need for bias stretch becomes an advantage.

In illustration (A) the position of maximum camber in this unstructured mainsail of the late 1970s is at around 50 per cent of the chord, indeed where it should always be on a two-sail rig. In the adjacent picture (B) the luff has been overtensioned on this same 35 foot boat by a mere 4 inches. The maximum camber point has now moved forward and vertical stretch lines have appeared along the luff somewhat similar to the creases in the handkerchief earlier.

The bias stretch of the panels at the luff, has allowed the weave under vertical tension to turn from squares to upright diamonds, pulling the camber towards the mast. What is not so obvious is that the increase in tension has set up a similar chain reaction along each panel stretching right back to the leech. Although nowhere near as obviously, the leech would have fallen off to lee-

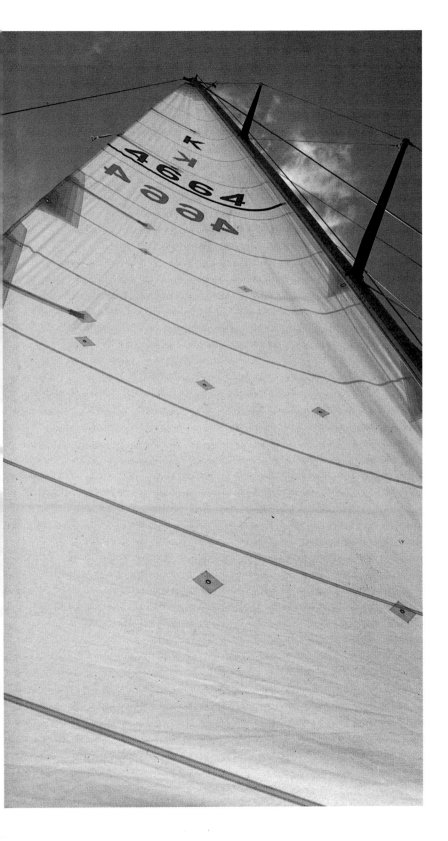

ward calling for an increase in downward tension via the main sheet.

Both illustrations, for reasons of clarity, were taken in the same wind strength, but had the wind increased after picture (B), it would have blown the maximum camber point back into the sail. The effect of increased luff and sheet tension would have been to return the maximum camber to its original position, at the same time as flattening the whole sail.

Camber depth

A similar system of control via bias stretch is used along the foot. The actual amount of vertical support given to the foot of the mainsail by the boom is very little. Its true role today is to give precise three-dimensional control of the clew position, both vertically and horizontally. The latter includes controlling the distance between the clew and luff of the sail, upon which depth of camber in the lower part of the sail depends.

The camber in a sail is put there either by excess luff curve, or as touched on earlier in the case of more structured cloth, by broadseaming. Whichever the method, the degree of camber can be measured as a ratio between the depth, at its maximum, and the width of the chord. Consequently for a given ratio, if the chord width is reduced the depth of camber will increase, and vice versa. In other words, if the distance between leech and luff is increased the sail will become flatter.

The fore and aft position of the clew along the boom does precisely this. It not only governs the chord length along the foot, but also, because it increases the distance between the clew and any point up the luff, it has an effect on the camber throughout the sail. This effect however diminishes with height. Look, nevertheless, at the effect relatively small differences in clew outhaul position have on the depth-to-chord ratio of this mainsail, again from the late 1970s, in these three pictures. Whilst not greatly noticeable from the cockpit, viewed from before the mast the relative fullness in each is obvious. Note too that the boom remains in each case at the same angle to the centreline.

Clew Cunningham

An extension of this range of control is the clew Cunningham or flattener. This is a cringle positioned a short distance up the leech at a point where, when brought to the black sail-area-limiting band on the boom, the lower camber in the sail would be flat enough for beating in winds up to the full mainsail limit, i.e. just before reefing becomes necessary.

In essence it allows the sail to stretch to the point where it is fully flattened, while remaining within the black band limit.

Foot shelves

The wedge shaped panels running along the foot are now superfluous. Their only use being, in lighter airs and when off the wind, to close the gap, between the straight boom and the adja-

(A) The clew outhaul is relaxed, adding fullness to the sail.

(B) With the foot stretched to its limit, depth is reduced.

(C) When the clew Cunningham or flattening reef is also taken in the sail becomes flatter still.

C ▶

From underneath the boom, the foot shelf in a mainsail is obvious.

cent camber in the sail.

Sails built in the 1970s favoured quite large foot shelves of this type. Their purpose was to provide an end-plate effect separating the flow on either side of a deeply cambered chord across the lower sail. This idea was questioned however, after lifting surface aerodynamic research showed that the high pressure flow across the windward surface of the main had an irresistible urge to migrate

under the boom toward the low pressure on the leeward side. The greater the depth-to-chord ratio, the greater was the urge; and the greater the trailing vortex formed by their resultant misbehaviour.

Ever since, the fashion for deep shelf foots has waned. This of course is quite separate from the more general principle that depth-to-chord ratios of all triangular sails gradually reduce from head to foot.

Up until this point the controls under review have been those applying to less structured

cloth constructions. The constan balancing of tensions along foo and luff and via the mainsheet while fine in theory, has sever drawbacks in practice. In parti cular, the compromises necessar to contain bias stretch in thes cloths, by balancing warp and fil yarns, severely limited the degre of control which could be exerte on the highly-loaded, and all important leech area.

Structured fabrics

Impregnation, *yarn temperin* and laminates have all steadily in creased the stability of sail cloth, and with each step forward, the degree to which tension can be balanced against stretch to achieve the right shape has steadily diminished. This is particularly true with headsails as will be seen. Mainsails, because of their need to adapt, still require adjustment but of a slightly different nature to their unstructured predecessors.

Mast bend

The answer is to use mast bend to increase the depth-to-chord ratios in those (upper) parts of the sail which the clew outhaul cannot reach. In fact of course, it is the same principle as before. Bowing the mast forward increases the chord of the sail and thereby reduces the camber. A side effect of mast bend incidentally is to reduce the distance between head and clew, thereby reducing tension on, and increasing twist in, the leech.

Any necessary positioning of the maximum camber is still controlled by luff tension but this in a structured sail is generally minimal anyway. So structured were the mainsails in use during the Freemantle America's Cup, that luff-long zippers were used to remove the excess cloth which on a conventional sail would be 'removed' by tightening either a halyard or luff Cunningham.

The more usual use of luff tension in structured sails is to iron out the diagonal creases which develop between the luff, at the point of maximum mast bend, and the clew.

Here is probably a relevant point to introduce the luff

Cunningham.

Luff Cunningham

The brainchild of Briggs Cunningham, it fulfils two functions.

Primarily it allows the mainsail to be cut to maximum luff dimensions for when that is most needed i.e. light airs. By introducing a Cunningham hole, or cringle, a short distance up the luff of the sail directly above the tack, tension can be applied to the luff to control maximum camber position when the wind pipes up. On small yachts it is usually only necessary to pass a line through

The fashion away from deep foot shelves is evident on this fractional rig racer. The foot chord is as flat as a board.

the sheave or hole and make it fast on the gooseneck. This provides a simple two-to-one purchase sufficient to allow tension to be adjusted easily and quickly. On larger yachts, and particularly those with structured sails, a larger purchase, or winch, will have to be incorporated.

The second advantage it bestows is that of being able to adjust luff tension without also having to adjust the mainsheet.

Because of the mainsail's triangular shape, apexing at the head, increased luff tension via the halyard also increases leech tension and reduces twist. The main sheet, controlling twist, has then also to be adjusted.

This neatly focuses attention once more on the leech and its vital role as the trailing edge of the headsail/mainsail combination.

Leech roach

Having wooed with a parallel and constant slot the slowing flow from the lee of the headsail to join the faster flow over its own lee, the main must then provide a flat efficient exit for both. The bogey to this is induced drag in the shape of tip vortices which form whenever high and low pressures meet. These are the trailing buckets that account for some 75 per cent of total rig drag.

It so happens that a triangular plan form with straight edges is the most efficient of tip vortex generators. A triangular mainsail with a straight leech would be just that, generating an unacceptably high drag to lift ratio.

It is also known, thanks to aerodynamicists like R. J. Mitchell who designed the Spitfire, that one way to reduce tip vortices is to introduce an elliptical curve into the trailing edge. Superimpose the outline of a Spitfire wing onto that of a modern mainsail with its elliptical roach, and the aerodynamic parentage of both becomes obvious. An elliptical trailing edge reduces the induced drag over that of a straight edged plan form by between 20 and 30 per cent.

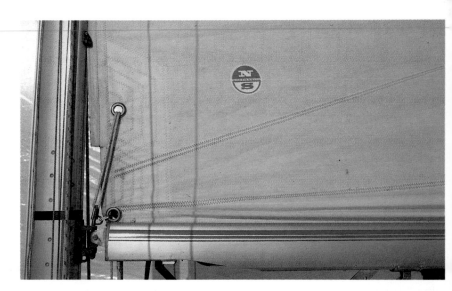

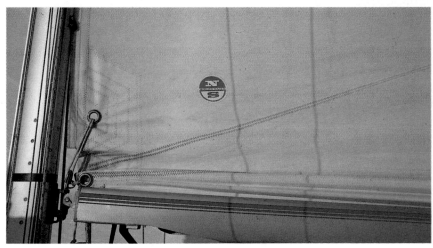

A simple purchase is all that is needed to control the luff Cunningham on this Half-Ton size boat.

Indeed, dipping below the water for a moment, that same elliptical shape provides more than a little insight into the origins of the increasingly fashionable keel shapes seen on current ocean racers. Remember, keels are beavering away below the surface generating lift, and drag, in exactly the same way as the sails above.

Battens

The leech roach therefore is a vital element in the fight against drag. However, to extend the leech into a convex curve calls for a framework of support. On a conventional mainsail this takes the form of battens. Usually four, their forward ends are aligned along the concave curve, or catenary, following the line of maximum tension between head and clew. Gaining their support from this they are able to extend the leech roach a distance outwards roughly equivalent to that between their inboard end and a straight line between head and clew. The catenary line trying, under tension, to straighten out, in effect pushes the battens aft, their outer ends taking the roach with them.

The desire for an even greater elliptical trailing edge can be seen in some of the sails driving boats not governed by class or IOR type rules. Modern high speed multi-hulls use full width battens which extend their roaches out into even tighter curves, in an effort to eliminate dragging tip vortices.

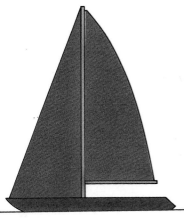

Left, the similarity between a mainsail roach and the aerodynamically-superb trailing edge of the Spitfire wing. ◄

▲
Above, the roach on a high-speed trimaran's fully-battened mainsail is even more similar. *Photo: Dave Blunden.*

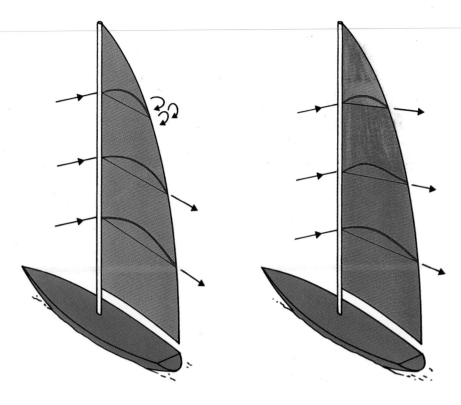

To prevent separation from the upper part of the sail, where the depth-to-chord ratio is greatest (left), the sail is twisted off, flattening the camber (right).

Twist

Whilst with tip vortices, and efforts to reduce their effect, a further word or two on twist. One thing is certain. A degree of twist in the upper part of a sail is beneficial. The question is why? More than one authority has explained the need for twist in terms of wind gradient – the boundary layer effect of the earth's surface on the wind blowing over it. According to this view, wind closer to the surface is slowed down by friction. There are many, including some scientists, with measurement on their side, who question this theory. The dif-

ferences in speed in the wind gradient at heights in which sails operate are very small indeed. For instance, a true wind at 6 feet above the sea blowing at 16.7 knots, would increase only to 18.2 knots at 20 feet and another 0.7 of a knot at 35 feet. Thereafter the increases are proportionally even less.

It is unlikely that when translated into apparent wind the small increase in velocity aloft would call for anything like the degree of twist which naturally falls into the upper part of a modern mainsail as the downward tensioning effect of the sheet diminishes.

The more likely explanation for the need for twist lies in two areas.

Were the depth-to-chord ratio high in the sail to be the same as lower down, the narrower chord would naturally generate less lift than in the lower, wider sections. In the case of the mainsail, foreshadowed by the influence of the mast, the surface area producing lift is also proportionally reduced as the sail narrows towards the head. The answer is for the designer to increase the depth-to-chord ratio as the sail narrows towards the head.

Were the angle of attack of the sail to remain constant, flow over the lee of the increased camber would not remain attached. Asked to turn and follow too sharp a curve the flow separates, stalling that part of the sail and generating drag. Consequently the angle of attack of that part of the sail has to be reduced. In other words twisted off.

Equally because the downwash from the reducing chord of the triangular headsail is lessened the nearer the head it gets, the wider the entry angle of the main needs to be. This again adds up to the need for twist aloft.

In the case of a fractional rig this need is even more apparent. The area of the main extending above the head of the jib is uninfluenced by any downwash. That portion of the sail has to be trimmed to the apparent wind at much the same angle as the foresail luff.

So much for twist, the elliptical roach and the contribution made by the main to the all important

▲
On rivers these Thames Raters for example, carry massive amounts of twist to catch the stronger breezes blowing above the tree-lined banks.

◄
The upper area of a fractional rig mainsail is uninfluenced by the circular flow effect from the jib.

slot. Luckily the practice has been made a darn sight easier to understand than the theory.

All of the numerical factors governing the optimum three dimensional shape of the sail should, as was seen in the chapter on design, have already been taken into account by the sailmaker. In other words, the elements within a good mainsail, once trimmed, should automatically interact to give an efficient shape. The simple aids to identifying correct trim will be detailed later.

However, the mainsail has to be very adaptable. It has to continue to work efficiently as the wind freshens to gale conditions, and must work well off the wind to provide maximum drive. If the sailmaker has really done his job properly the necessary elements to provide the wide spectrum of adjustment needed to meet these challenges will also have been incorporated within the structure. Nevertheless the onus is on the sailor to do the adjusting to balance the varying forces on the sail with the controls he has to hand.

Reefing

As the wind strength increases so the forces generated by the sails increase proportionally. Unfortunately when working to windward, resistance on the hull of the boat soon wastes the small proportion of increased forward drive. This is exacerbated by the increase of drag over lift generated by the full depth to chord ratio in the sail. The large proportion of sideways force however builds unhindered, and counteracted only by the static righting moment of the keel, the boat heels.

The answer is to reduce the plan form of the sail, but equally at the same time the camber within has to be flattened in order to reduce the increased drag.

The need to shorten sail in a blow is a fundamental recognised by all sailors. Strangely, the need to flatten the sail at the same time is less so. Roller reefing, for

example, was for many years a popular and relatively easy method of reducing mainsail area. The flaw in the system was that there was no provision for increasing the chord of the sail, and so reducing its camber. In fact as the sail was wound down around the boom, the leech was drawn forward by the pressure within the sail, actually increasing its depth-to-chord ratio.

Slab

The answer, almost universally adopted for the modern mainsail, is to combine the clew Cunningham principle used to flatten the full size sail, with the slab reefing system used by our grandfathers.

The sail is equipped with luff and leech cringles set into reinforced 'corner' panels at each reef point. Simple hooks to take alternate luff cringles are incorporated on the gooseneck, and two pennants are led from the inner end of the boom, where they are always within reach, out to adjustable fairleads on either side of the outer boom end. From there they are passed up through alternate leech cringles and then back down again to be secured on the boom.

There are a number of variations but whatever the detail, the aim is the same. When reefed the direction of the two part purchase reaching up to the cringle should follow an imaginary line between the clew and a point midway up the luff of the sail. Only in this way will the vertical and horizontal pull on the sail, once the reef is taken in, provide the balanced

Fully-battened cruising mainsails make reefing and sail-shape control much easier. *Photo: North Sails Inc.*

By far the most efficient reefing system is the modern slab, which reduces area and depth-to-chord ratio simultaneously. The camber in this flattened mainsail has almost disappeared behind the mast.

force necessary to flatten the whole sail. Apart from distorting its designed optimum shape when reefed, there is a real danger that too much pull in one direction could stretch and permanently damage the sail. Once the correct positions for each reef are established, the adjustable leads, or stops, can be fixed.

In operation, reefing is then simplicity itself. The main halyard is eased to the point where the luff cringle can be hooked to the gooseneck and then retensioned. It is important that this is done before strain comes on the reefing line, as the luff could otherwise be pulled from its track. The reefing line can then be winched in pulling the outer end of the boom and the leech cringle together. Finally, the halyard tension is adjusted to position the maximum depth of camber.

In mainsails made from more structured materials it will also be necessary to increase mast bend to flatten further the depth-to-chord ratio in the upper part of the sail.

This simple system provides an extremely efficient method of utilising the qualities which the sailmaker has designed into the sail from the outset. Compare the flattened camber of the reefed mainsail viewed from in front of the mast, with those of unreefed sails on page 68. The sail is almost hidden behind the mast.

Reefing lines

As the reefed sail is flattened

throughout by tension between clew and luff, the horizontal row of small reefing cringles set into the sail become superfluous to 'tying down a reef'. Indeed, excess vertical tension on them could cause permanent distortion to the adjacent cloth. They should be used only to tidy up the excess fold of sail along the top of the boom. Conventionally this is rolled up and secured with short lengths of line, run through each cringle and tied underneath the boom.

As these can rarely be found when needed, an alternative is one long length which can be secured at the gooseneck and laced through each cringle and under the boom in a series of half-hitches.

Roller furling/reefing

Inspired no doubt by the understandable success of roller reefing for headsails, a similar concept has been harnessed to stow and reef the mainsail.

There are a number of systems available employing a grooved-luff foil, either inside or immediately aft of the mast. When rotated this foil rolls the sail up around itself for stowing. 'Hoisting', if this is the right word, is accomplished by pulling out the clew and allowing the foil to rotate in the opposite direction. As with modern roller reefing headsail systems, the hardware is substantial enough to withstand the strains from a partially unrolled sail when reefed.

Even though the mainsail area is therefore infinitely adjustable, it would appear that this is not seen

The roller furling main is certainly ship-shape and Bristol fashion when stowed.

by many as the primary benefit from the system. The ease with which the sail can be got ready, hoisted and eventually stowed, carries more weight. Against this, are the extra expense, weight and complication of gear which might fail or jam; but perhaps that is a discussion for another place. Here the subject is sails.

For roller furling mainsails the problem is two fold. Obviously if the sail is going to be stowed around a narrow foil, the traditional horizontal battens have to be dispensed with. With the battens go the roach, and without the roach, drag in the form of a trailing vortex returns in strength. The leech of most sails of this type is actually cut slightly concave to avoid curl. The soft vertical battens on some sails allow this concave leech to be straightened. In no way will they support a roach.

The other side of the performance problem is along the foot. If the sail is to be rolled it becomes impractical to attach it to the boom along the length of its foot. The single point attachment at the clew gives good camber shape control, but the gap between foot and boom allows high pressure flow to migrate from the windward side to the low pressure area to leeward. The result is another swirling vortex. Performance is not improved.

Off the wind

Very little attention has been paid so far to anything other than the how and why of going to windward. Yet for many recreational sailors that is the least at-

tractive point on which to spend their weekend's effort. It even used to be said of sailors from a more leisured age that 'gentlemen do not sail to windward'.

The lack of roach and the gap between the foot and the boom, when set, are evident on Round the World winner, *Flyer*, now re-rigged for cruising. *Photo: Nick Rains/ PPL*

The reason why little space is devoted to off wind sailing, at least that without spinnakers, is that there is not much to say about it. Certainly very little research has been devoted to unravelling its finer mysteries. Maybe the attitude is summed up in the term 'a soldier's wind', i.e. anyone can sail a boat once the wind frees. Although why that branch of the armed services deserves the compliment pales when one recalls the three most useless things on a sailing boat, according to the facetious, are: a wheelbarrow, a step ladder and a navy officer.

Perhaps a return to a more scientific arena is called for. On the wind, it will be remembered, most of the force generated by the sail's aerofoils was sideways, working against the righting moment of the keel, and across the direction of travel. From this a small forward component of lift could be extracted but this was in turn diluted by a countering drag force. To optimise forward lift, the drag generated over the aerofoil had to be reduced.

Once off the wind and the sheets eased the same forces are there, but their inter-relationship has changed.

Now the side force component has swung around more in line with the direction of travel. As the sheets are eased further the total force generated by the sail will move forward until the sail reaches a point where it can no longer bend the wind across its lee surface. During this phase lift generated by the sail is working more and more directly against the drag

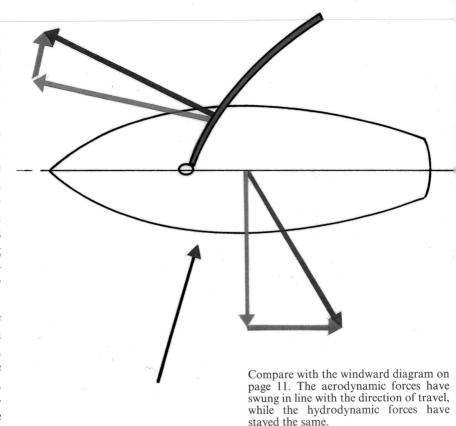

Compare with the windward diagram on page 11. The aerodynamic forces have swung in line with the direction of travel, while the hydrodynamic forces have stayed the same.

A soldier's wind. *Photo: Rick Tomlinson/ PPL* ▶

forces on the underwater hull.

Equally, the drag forces generated as a by-product of lift, and from the form and friction of the rig, are swinging further and further around until they become a sideways component, heeling the boat by working against the righting moment of the keel. In practice every sailor knows what happens. Once off the wind, the boat picks up speed and gradually heel is reduced.

Not quite as obviously, the upwash effect of the main on the foresail, and the downwash of the latter on the former are gradually reduced as their individual circulatory systems draw apart.

What then does this mean in terms of the mainsail?

Attack angle

Primarily it means that the mainsail should be angled across the wind as far forward as is possible. This will align the direction of lift with that of travel. The limiting factor to increasing the angle of the sail with the centreline is that point when the flow no longer has to bend around its leeward surface. A circular flow is not established and pressure on either side of the luff remains equal. In other words, the luff flutters.

The opposite effect, when the sail is angled too closely to the centreline and flow separates

across the whole of the lee surface because it was asked to bend at too great an angle, is not so apparent on a mainsail due to the mast shadowing the luff area. More of this when tell-tales are discussed in the pages following.

In practice the main can be angled to the point just before the pressure on the forward half of the sail equalises, i.e. luffs; and of course this angling of the sail to the wind is controlled with the mainsheet.

The mainsheet, once eased, has very little control over the after half of the sail. Its downward component is only effective whilst the boom is directly above its lower fixing point on the deck, or if fitted, the leeward end of the mainsheet track. Without a downward force, as the boom swings outboard it will lift, allowing the leech of the sail to twist off to leeward.

Vang

Excess twist, both reduces lift generating camber, and towards the head will allow the whole chord of the sail to increase its angle of attack, and luff. Lift at the head will be reduced and eventually lost altogether.

Obviously some vertical control of the boom, and therefore the leech of the sail, has to be introduced, and this is provided by the kicking strap, or vang.

The vang, whether it be a simple purchase, cam-lever, solid spar with screw adjustment or hydraulic ram, has other roles to play on performance boats particularly in windward work, but its primary use is to control boom height and therefore leech ten-

81

This vang combines a purchase down-haul with a simple solid strut. The latter is useful for increasing mainsail twist and keeping the boom horizontal when reefing.

The French-made Walder boom brake incorporates a friction clutch. As well as acting as a vang, it provides total control of the boom during a gybe.

sion once the boat is off the wind. That the leech can be controlled precisely is important, and to see why, back for a moment to aerodynamics.

With a freeing wind it is just as important that the flow should exit efficiently from the leech of the main. Countering this is the need to generate as much lift in as

forward a direction as possible. The latter calls for an increased depth-to-chord ratio in the mainsail, achieved by easing the clew outhaul or reducing the mast bend, or more usually a combination of both. In each case the leech will tighten, with a consequent increase in drag, now increasing the heel of the boat. Some twist must be induced in the sail if the boat is to remain as upright, and therefore as efficient, as possible.

On a close reach, with the sheets just cracked, the mainsail with its controlling boom is a much greater lift generator than the foresail. This is particularly true of large overlapping genoas, which unable to be angled accurately to the freeing wind, lose lift at the direct expense of drag.

This, countered against the lift of the more efficient main, can exert a significant force on the lateral balance of the boat. Considerable lee rudder, with a consequent increase in underwater drag, is necessary to counter the weather helm and keep the boat tracking in a straight line.

Before the wind

Once the wind passes aft of the beam the mainsail is presented with quite a different set of circumstances.

As the wind draws aft the importance of the main in the two sail equation becomes paramount. Indeed, on a run, it completely shadows a foresail left on the leeward side.

More fundamentally, the main can no longer hope to bend the wind around its luff, inducing

lift on its leeward surface. The angle is now just too great.

Aerodynamically drag almost completely supersedes lift within the equation, and it is therefore to the production of the greatest amount of drag possible that the sailor must turn.

What forces that can be generated by flow across the sail are

On the left, the tight leech of the mainsail inhibits efficient circular flow. On the right, depth-to-chord ratio has been reduced by twisting off the leech to match that of the headsail.

Downwind twist in the leech is inefficient. On the left, the leech is spilling flow. On the right, the vang has been hardened down, tightening the leech.

limited to an increase in positive pressure on the windward surface, and those marginal areas of low pressure that can be encouraged around the edges of the triangular plan form. In otherwords the efficient airofoil must now be made as inefficient a flow generator as possible. Camber at both leech and luff must now be deepened, both to gather and slow down flow on the windward surface,

and, by so doing, increase the area of resistance. Drag inducing vortices are thrown out on either side of the sail.

To achieve this section, the depth-to-chord ratio is increased by easing the clew outhaul right off. Maximum camber position is allowed to sink back into the sail, and the leech is hardened by tensioning the vang. It is possible, if pivot centres of gooseneck and vang on the mast are not aligned, that tension on the vang actually restricts squaring the boom across the wind. In such cases the need to get the boom square takes priority

over leech shape.

Leech line

There is one final control built into the mainsail for just this point of sailing. During manufacture, a light chord is run inside the tabling around the eliptical curve of the roach between head and clew. Conventionally it will be fixed at the head, exiting around a lead at the clew and then running along the boom to the gooseneck where it can always be reached. More recently a variation has appeared. The clew end is attached, and the line, exiting at

The purchase needed to harden the leech line on a large mainsail is substantial.

Viewed from the side the camber in this mainsail resembles that of a very flat spinnaker. The leech is tight, and the body of the sail is converting the following wind into drag.

the head, is led around a turning block and thence down the luff to the gooseneck. Either way the end is the same.

Under tension the leech line between the head and clew will try to straighten out, hooking the elliptical roach of the sail to windward and deepening the camber of the sail up and down its after edge.

For the sailor content to sail down wind without a spinnaker, a mainsail so shaped is the very next best thing.

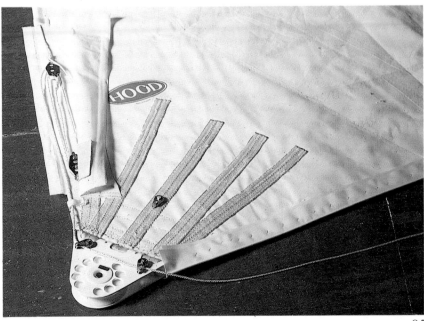

▼ The purchase needed to harden the leech line on a large mainsail is substantial.

85

Foresails

In any multi-sail rig beating to windward, the sail in front is the most important. Not only is the total force per square foot one and a half times that of the sail behind it, the proportion of lift in the direction of travel is significantly greater than that making the boat heel.

All of these qualities derive from the circular flow generated around the mainsail and its effect on that circulating around the foresail. The main becomes less efficient, but at the same time improves that of the foresail by freeing its apparent wind.

What roles therefore is the foresail called upon to play?

As the leading edge of the combination it has to bend the flow arriving to windward around its forward edge and keep it attached along its leeward surface. In doing so it will not only maximise the circulation, and therefore drive, around itself, it will increase the circular flow around the main, which in turn frees the apparent wind in which the foresail is operating.

The desire for more lift from the efficient sounding headsail, has of course as always to be tempered by the need to limit drag. Asking flow to bend too steeply around the camber of the foresail both reduces lift and increases pressure drag.

Both the position of maximum camber and the depth-to-chord ratio must be able to be adjusted. The degree necessary however is much less than within the mainsail. In an increasing wind for example, a foresail can be changed to one of less area and of flatter section.

The contribution made by the foresail sadly diminishes as the wind frees. On a reach it is still possible to exert sufficient control over its shape to produce a degree of lift, but as the wind frees further the proportion is rapidly eroded by increasing amounts of drag. Flow over the lee surface separates earlier and earlier. On these points of sailing lift is thankfully in the direction of travel. The resultant increase in drag is equally thankfully only contributing to heel.

The relative inefficiency of the foresail to the mainsail while reaching is at its most obvious on boats carrying large overlapping genoas. Unlike the main, the shape of which can, via the boom, be controlled on all points of sailing, sheeting limitations imposed by deck mounted fairleads severely restrict efficient camber control of genoas once the wind frees.

Whilst reaching in a breeze the foresail may appear the all powerful. In fact lift is more than offset by the drag generated, and it is the main from which the real driving force stems. So much so that quite large lumps of weather helm are needed to counteract the imbalance created by the relative efficiency of the two sails.

Once before the wind the foresail suffers even greater indignities. As the wind moves aft it is blanketed more and more by the mainsail. Until it can be set on the opposite side of the boat (goose-winged) it is contributing very little to the overall drive picture.

Fairly obvious therefore that it is when contributing to windward efficiency that the headsail, or foresail, finds itself in its element.

Photo: Rick Tomlinson/PPL

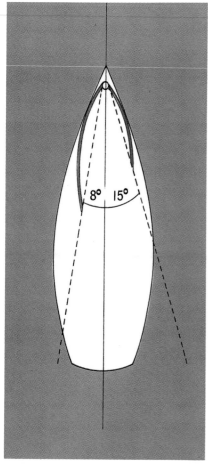

For similar angles of attack, the sheeting angle is directly proportional to the length of chord.

Leading edge

In order to re-establish the importance of the foresail in the total equation it is worthwhile looking again at how flow approaches the leading edge.

The circular flow which becomes established around a single foil bends the wind towards the leading edge before it actually reaches it. This is upwash. When two foils, or sails, are interacting, the circular flow around the after, or mainsail, increases the amount

88

of upwash approaching the luff of the foresail by increasing its apparent speed. The apparent wind direction is drawn aft and the foresail effectively gets a lift.

The benefits of this are two fold.

Angle of attack

First and most important, the angle between the chord of the sail and the centreline of the boat can be increased. The total force (lift and drag) generated by the headsail correspondingly swivels forward more in line with the direction the boat wants to go. Forward drive is increased and sideways heel is reduced.

This increased angle of attack for a foresail, compared to that of the main, sheeted on or close to the centreline, can be quite large. It increases for smaller foresails in proportion to their chord and depth of camber. For similar angles of attack at the luff, a full size overlapping genoa would typically make a chord/centreline angle of 8 degrees, compared to some 15 degrees for a non-overlapping jib.

Depth of camber

The second benefit lies in the degree of camber which can be incorporated in the foresail. It has been established that the depth to chord ratio of any sail directly governs the lift to drag ratio.

The increased angle of attack of the foresail allows the depth-to-chord ratio to be increased, with a subsequent rise in generated lift. The same angle, more across the

wind than the main, decreases the chance of separation taking place. The ratio of lift to drag despite the increase in camber remains on the plus side.

A depth-to-chord ratio of up to 18 per cent is quite likely in the upper part of a full size masthead genoa, compared to say 14 per cent at the same height on a modern main. As headsail size decreases, so does the depth-to-chord ratio. A flat low-aspect jib for example, would be similar to a mainsail in camber depth. Very high aspect ratio blade jibs on the other hand have much higher ratios due to their shorter chords aloft.

Of course, depth-to-chord ratios are indivisible from that old friend, twist. In an earlier chapter it was established that the primary reason for building twist into triangular sails was to allow greater, or deeper, lift producing cambers as the sail narrows towards its apex. If separation is not to occur over the more acute leeward curve, the angle of attack has to be progressively increased near the head of the sail.

The degree of twist in a headsail has to be greater than that built into the mainsail. Unlike the main, the headsail does not benefit from a sail ahead of it bending the flow back across its leeward surface. Were flow, already subject to a relatively sharp bend around the headsail luff, to separate early, the total power producing leeward flow over both sails would be compromised.

The need to match the camber in the forward body of the main to the twisted leech of the headsail was discussed in the previous chapter. This of course is the other vital element in achieving an extended flow across both sails.

On fractionally rigged boats this calls for an even greater degree of twist in the headsail. Not only does the fractional headsail narrow at a level at which the mainsail is much fuller in section, but it does so when the upwash from the wider chord of the mainsail is also greater. This disproportionate freeing of the apparent wind calls for more twist to be designed into the headsail, reducing the depth-to-chord ratio to, typically, around 12 per cent.

The simple North Sailscope gives a fair indication of both depth-to-chord ratio, and more usefully, the position of maximum camber depth.

Aerodynamics account for only a few of the ways in which a headsail differs from a mainsail. The factor exerting the greatest effect is the absence of a rigid boom providing support along the foot.

Support in tension

Turning again to a stress map, this time of a medium aspect headsail, a similar pattern of isostatic load lines paint a picture close to that of the mainsail. However, there are differences. Whilst the sail is held in tension between the same three points, tack, head and clew, support for both leech and foot is totally dependent on tension at one point—the clew.

With support only along one side of the sail, i.e. that provided by the forestay to the luff, inward collapse along both the foot, and more importantly, the leech is only restricted by tension from a sheet bisecting the angle at the clew. This not only provides problems of trim for the sailor, but over the years some considerable heartache for the sailmaker.

Of the two unsupported edges, that with the highest loading is the leech, running across the direction of flow. It is also the longer of the two. Obviously that was the edge along which to line up the more resistant fill threads. Sadly this meant that the panels met the foot, as well as the luff, across the bias. Fine for the latter, supported by the headstay, but not so good for the former. Twenty years ago the only answer was to divide the sail in two, lining

up fill threads along both foot and leech, with the panels meeting each other in the body of the sail, along what was known as the mitre line.

Few, if any, mitre-cut sails are made today, but thanks to the longevity of *Dacron* there are many still in use.

It was the arrival of more structured weaves in the late 70s which retired the mitre-cut to its place in history. Since then, steady improvements in design and manufacturing control have produced weaves with sufficient structure in themselves to withstand collapse along the foot, whilst sailmaking techniques, such as two-plying the leech have given even greater control on that critical area.

Of course, the drive for improvement in materials has not been solely motivated by headsail foot collapse. The higher structural integrity of modern fabrics has made its presence felt throughout the headsail.

Although the greatest loadings are along the leech, they are not as disproportionate as with, for example, those of a high aspect main. At the same time high value is placed on low bias stretch. As was seen earlier this is best achieved by a balanced weave where fill equals warp and crimp is even. *Dacron* headsail fabrics, other than for blade jibs and the like, are therefore of this so-called

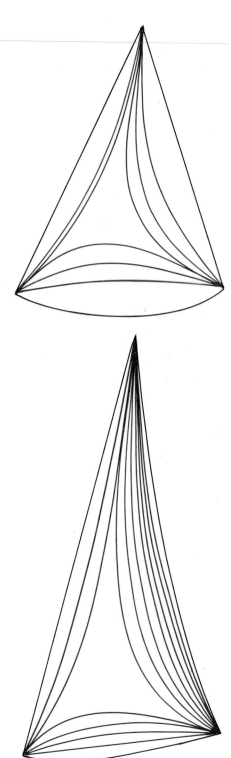

Top, the isostatic stress lines in a medium aspect headsail are more balanced than those of a mainsail. As the aspect ratio increases (below), the load lines along the leech more approximate those in a mainsail.

balanced weave. In laminate sails, where bias stretch is restricted by the film, a variety of reinforcements are incorporated to counteract leech loadings, similar in fashion to those in mainsails.

The limited range factors

One basic difference exists between headsails and the mainsail. Each of the former has to work within only a fraction of the total wind range with which the latter is obliged to cope. This immediately reduces the degree of adjustability necessary in each particular headsail.

Fashions ebb and flow in sails as in most other areas. Early *Dacron* sails were simply synthetic versions of traditional sail cloth, their shape dictated by a wire luff rope, which when set up hard limited any further control over the degree or position of camber within the sail. For racing, a wide range of headsails was carried.

The stretch luff tape was substituted solely to allow some control over the shape of the sail in varying wind conditions, but since then each step in the material evolution has been aimed at reducing the need to adjust tensions within the headsail.

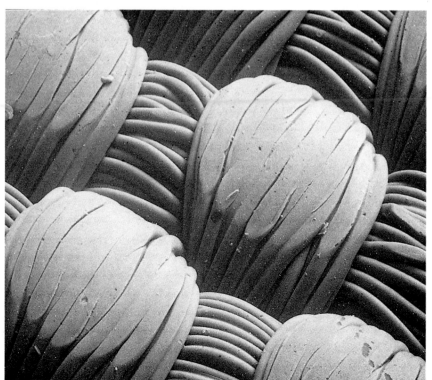

The *Dacron* weave (above left) for a lightweight medium aspect crosscut headsail is much more balanced than that of the earlier mainsail. The fill yarns, although heavier than the warps, are more sharply crimped. To the same × 80 scale, the weave for a heavier high aspect headsail (below) sees the fill yarns straightening out again to combat high leech loads.

91

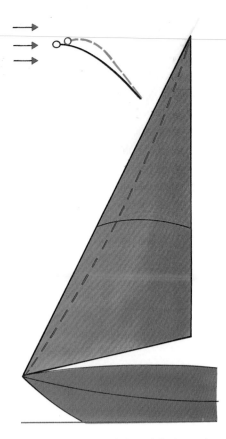

As the luff sags (red dotted line), so the depth-to-chord ratio increases (from black solid to dotted green).

Three pictures on page 95 show maximum depth position adjustment via luff tension on a 1977 unstructured *Dacron* headsail. The range of halyard adjustment from draft-forward to draft-aft was roughly 12 inches. A similar range with an early laminate sail, of say five years later, would be a quarter of this, and five years after that the latest state-of-the-art laminate headsail would hardly respond to differing halyard tension at all.

The march of progress has of course not been in reducing control as an end in itself. It has been to produce sails which are stable enough not to be distorted by changes in the wind strength or boat speed. In the limited wind band in which headsails have to work, that goal is now a reality for sailors in the vanguard of the racing fleets. For others patiently trying to wear out their existing sails, shape control is here to stay for some little while yet.

Luff

Even though it provides a measure of support to the headsail's luff, the forestay is materially quite different to the more solid and stable mast section supporting the mainsail.

Under load from the sail the flexible forestay will sag. It is practically impossible to eliminate this sag completely, although there are a number of ways in which it can be minimised, and even more important, controlled.

As will become clear when attention is turned later to sail trim, luff sag has emerged as an important avenue towards effective camber control. Only achievable however, if the degree of sag can be consistently controlled by the sailor, an aspect of rig tuning touched upon later.

The principle on offer therefore is that luff sag is no bad thing, provided:
a) it is under control, and,
b) the sailmaker understands before the sail is cut what degree will remain when the rig is under maximum tension.
Only with this knowledge can the luff curve of the sail be cut to compensate effectively for whatever sag will remain in the stay when wind conditions are near the sail's upper limit. It is then that sag is at its most counterproductive. As the wind and sag increase, so the luff is blown back towards the leech, reducing the chord and deepening the camber. Exactly the opposite effect to that needed.

Foil or hanks?

Whilst with the luff it is worth examining the various pros and cons of the methods for attaching headsail to forestay. Leaving aside for the moment roller-reefing systems, about which more anon, the argument boils down between the traditional hanks and a forestay-length grooved extrusion into which is fed a latterday fine plastic version of the bolt-rope. It is a miniature version of the mainsail luff groove system fitted on many masts.

Aerodynamically the argument is more finely balanced than one might think. Whilst the head-foil is invariably bulkier and should therefore increase drag because it is aerodynamically considered as one with the hoisted sail, the proportion of drag attributable to the foil is dramatically reduced. Indeed, when measured as one, the drag generated by the headfoil is much less than that generated by a circular sectioned wire or rod forestay, even though the latter is a fraction of the diameter.

Where aerodynamic doubt remains is whether when hanks are used, because of the forestay's close proximity to the sail's leading edge, the same criteria apply

92

In truth the only reason amongst performance sailors for the almost universal adoption of headfoils is for changing sails. With twin grooves in the foil, a new headsail can be hoisted before the old sail is lowered. On the race circuits, bareheaded changes are a thing of the past.

Returning again for a moment to the aerodynamics, there is another reason why there can be little benefit in one over the other. At the very edge of the luff, flow is separated anyway.

The great attraction of foil headstays is the elimination of bare-headed sail changes ...

... although the traditional hank will keep the lowered sail attached to the boat.

as that used for calculating headfoil drag. If it does, and no one actually has any hard proof, then the drag from a hanked on headsail would be very much less than that using a headfoil system; however efficient and aerodynamic the latter might appear.

There is no argument over which system is the more convenient and handy to use. The hanks win hands down. When the sail is lowered it remains firmly attached to the vessel, from where it can be safely secured along the deck until it is either raised again, or stowed below. Again, a hanked foresail can be hoisted by one man. A foil system needs at least two; one to control and feed in the luff tape, another to haul on the halyard.

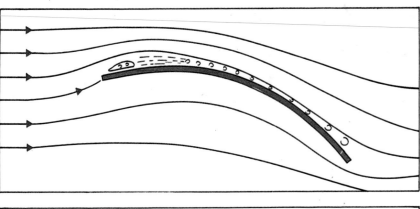

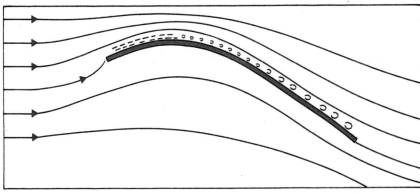

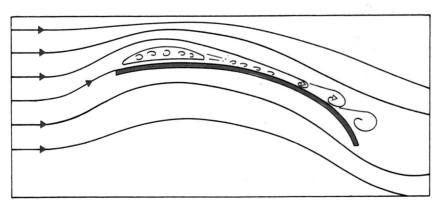

recalled this is the highly efficient, rarely achieved type of flow. Bearing in mind the sail's surface, its mobile form and structure, and the general bounce of the boat itself, laminar flow is understandably elusive.

From well forward of the maximum depth of camber, laminar flow will have become turbulent. This is still producing power and is far less liable to separate. Remember it is separation that must be guarded against at all costs as the low pressure fast flow slows down into the high pressure misbehaviour zone. Before separation is allowed to happen, relatively fast low-pressure flow across the lee of the main attracts it sufficiently to make the jump across the slot, so extending its power producing run.

Examine then how three sections (left), each with a differing position for maximum depth will influence the flow. At the top maximum depth is around 45 per cent, roughly where aerodynamicists and sailmakers agree is the ideal position for a powerful smoothwater headsail.

The sharp turn demanded of the air flow has inevitably formed a separation bubble forward, and the relatively rapid decline in camber aft of maximum depth is tempting the flow to misbehave into separation or drag. Any deviation in wind speed or direction of the boat's course will either feather the sail to windward or widen the forward separation bubble. This could lead to total separation to leeward. In racing vernacular the boat is beating in a very narrow groove. In the centre picture max-

Headsail flow

It will be remembered that an aerofoil introduced at an angle into a flow actually bends that flow towards its leading edge.

So sharply is this flow required to bend up and around the headsail luff that it gives up once just around the corner. A small

'bubble' of separated air forms just behind the leeward luff. To a greater or lesser degree it is probably always there whilst driving to windward. The width of the bubble is however controllable.

Aft of the bubble the air reattaches itself for a relatively short period as laminar flow. It will be

94

mum depth has been pulled forward, at the same time flattening
the leech. The leading edge bubble
has disappeared as the camber has
moved forward, softening the
sharp bend. Past the point of maximum depth the relatively flat section reduces the likelihood of low
pressure rapidly swirling into high
pressure drag. However, the increased forward camber on the
windward side will reduce the
angle at which the boat will point.
The groove is wide and forgiving,
and as will be seen when trim is
discussed, ideal for beating in
anything less than perfect sea
conditions.

So far both shapes, in the right
sailing conditions have much to
be said for them. Aerodynamically speaking the third (lower) is all
bad.

Maximum draft is now well
aft of mid chord and the forward
part of the sail, the entry, is very
flat. This condition is common in
headsails made from early unstructured fabrics, when as the
wind increases, little or no attention is paid to luff tension. By
ignoring the need to balance the
extra weight of wind in the sail
with additional luff tension, the
camber in the sail has been, literally, blown aft.

Flow around the luff finds it
impossible to turn the corner and
a large separation bubble is established. What little attached flow
that remains over the vital forward facing half of the sail is minimised in effect due to the relative
flatness of the section; and lift is
almost all in a sideways direction.
The relatively sharp camber aft
also heightens the chance of sep-

The three pictures show the shapes in
practise. Above the camber is correct for
high pointing in smooth water. Top right,
it is too far forward, even for heavy sea
sailing; and bottom right, it has been
blown aft.

aration once flow has passed the
point of lowest pressure, compromising in turn the chances of an
efficient jump across the slot onto
the mainsail. All in all, there is absolutely nothing to be said for it,
and that is as true for the leisurely
cruiser as it is for an out-and-out
racer.

Curled leech

There are some parallels with the above draft-aft condition and the curled, or hard, leech to which all sails eventually succumb. Of course the detrimental effect on total lift/drag is nowhere near the same as with the more general draft-aft trim described before.

The most usual cause for a leech curling to windward is the tabling, or hem, sewn into the sail to eliminate fraying. This double or triple thickness of fabric stretches less than the cloth it borders. In time, the loading on the leech causes this adjacent fabric to yield permanently.

Recognising this eventuality, the sailmaker allows some give in the tabling during manufacture; at the same time providing a leech line with which consequential flutter can be tensioned once the sail is set.

Unfortunately stretch in the adjacent fabric, sooner or later, catches up with the allowance made. Then the only solution is for the sail to be returned to the maker for the seams in the adjacent fabric to be taken up. It is remarkable how few sails go back for this simple and inexpensive operation. Some idea of the effect on performance, and indeed the importance some sailors place on a curl-free leech, can be gleaned from the experience of keen racing sailors. Amongst that body it is not unusual for a favourite headsail to be returned for a little leech surgery every two months during the racing season.

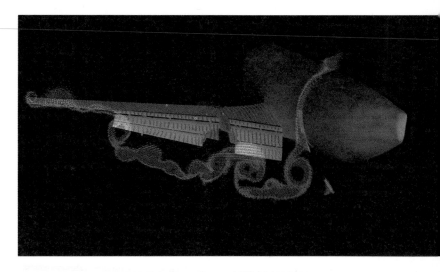

A laser beam is used to highlight vortices caused by the flaps of a new Boeing jet liner. On a smaller scale, a curled headsail leech generates the same dragging effect.

A headsail which touches the deck (left) is aerodynamically as viable as on an aircraft wing. The mainsail (right) is much harder to evaluate.

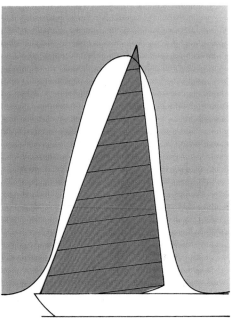

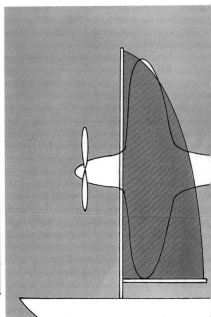

Foot

It will be recalled that the trend in mainsails over recent years has been to flatten the camber towards the foot. The idea, first formulated from lifting surface studies and subsequently proved on the race courses, stemmed from a need to reduce the pressure ratios on either side of the mainsail in an area where high pressure could migrate to low pressure by swirling underneath the boom. The eventual aim was to reduce the effect of an energy-sapping trailing vortex forming at the foot of the sail as well as at the head.

Ironically, that same lifting surface theory, together with advances in fabric integrity, has led the way to increases in camber, or depth-to-chord ratios, along the foot of headsails.

For the reasoning it is necessary to go back to the aircraft wing analogy. Because of the gap between the foot of a mainsail and the deck of the boat, aerodynamicists had to consider the mainsail as a total wing span. An aircraft wing has, after all, no gap between its root and the fuselage. A headsail on the other hand approximates much closer to a single wing, as long as the foot can be sealed along the deck of the boat. If, and it is a big if, this can be achieved, high pressure flow along the windward surface is contained, and cannot swirl underneath to compromise the low pressure lift producing flow to leeward. A trailing vortex from the headsail clew is stunted.

To be effective the foot of the sail, to at least the mid-chord, must be in physical contact with the deck, which severely restricts visibility. Not so much of a problem with see-through laminate sails!

The big if comes in because if the seal is to work, it has to be total. The foot of the sail has to make a physical join with the deck. This of course is the origin, and sustenance over recent years, of the deck-sweeping genoa.

However true the theory—and there are some interesting counter-arguments around—for most sailors the added efficiency of the deck sweeping foot is far outweighed by other considerations.

Deck-sweepers are fine for fully crewed racing yachts with plenty of folk on board to keep a lookout on behalf of the half-blinded helmsman. For most sailors a foot cut higher makes for more confident seamanship. The overall dimensions of headsails also limit the degree by which the foot can be cut parallel to the deck. As the aspect ratio increases so the clew must be raised.

For the increasingly popular roller-reefing headsail, a deck-sweeping foot is impracticable anyway. As will be seen later, such a shape would compromise both furling and sheet lead efficiency.

Purpose-built racing machines are already softening the deck edge to reduce vortices climbing aboard.

Enough interest in such phenomena is already resulting in an increasing number of attempts on dedicated racing craft to soften the hull/deck edge. If the theory can be proved in practice, the end is in sight for the deck-scraper. With low pressure on either side of the foot there is no point in continuing with their inconvenience.

Following the theory through, the mischievous might also dare question another sacred cow. If a sharp deck edge results in an energy sapping vortex worth talking about, what is the effect from the massed ranks of an ocean racing crew all sitting out along the windward rail?

Headsail control

Due largely to the relatively narrow wind strength bands within which each headsail has to work, the number of controls over its shape are few compared with those for the mainsail. This is particularly true when talking about the latest generation of *yarn tempered* and laminate constructions. Once set up, within their designed balances, there is little call for further, or constant, adjustment.

Later in the section on trim, control over headsail shape by forestay and luff tension will enter the picture. However, at this stage, whilst discussing fundamentals applicable to all boats and all sailors, there is one control which needs to be addressed.

Unlike the mainsail, the only counter-balance to tension between head and tack of the headsail comes from the sheet attached to a single clew point. Conseq-

Deck vortex

As the concepts of vortices crystallise in sailing terms, there is one that could pour water on

Nevertheless the idea is well established, particularly among the performance-minded. On the horizon, however, there is a morsal of food for thought which might just change the whole approach.

more than one sacred cow. Wind at sea level meeting the topsides of a boat reacts in manner similar to that meeting the sails. In this case it is forced up and over the deck. As it does it increases in speed and separates over the sharp hull/deck edge. Immediately, so the theory goes, it forms a high speed vortex swirling across and into the windward surface of a deck-scraping genoa, cancelling out any slow moving high pressure flow, before exiting through the slot.

uently any misalignment of the angle at which the sheet exerts a force on the clew will unbalance the entire sail. It is fundamental therefore to understand and maintain the correct angle, not only to windward, but also when the wind frees.

Sheeting angle

The easiest way to understand the effect of sheeting angle is to think of the entire headsail rocking on an imaginary point roughly midway up the luff.

If the sheet is angled to exert more downward pull than is necessary, the top of the sail will rock backwards. The angle of attack above the mid luff will decrease progressively towards the head and twist in the upper half will diminish. This in turn will deepen the depth-to-chord ratio. By the same token the relative lack of tension along the lower half of the sail will increase the angle of at-

tack of the lower luff. Because the clew is moved closer to the tack, the depth-to-chord ratio in the lower part of the sail also increases.

On a performance boat there is a case for such a move, for instance as the wind lightens.

The reverse happens if the sheet exerts too much horizontal pull, as when the lead is too far aft. The upper part of the sail now rocks forward, increasing the attack angle. The lower part flattens and the angle of attack progressively decreases down to the tack.

How then to determine the correct sheeting angle?

Many modern headsails made today incorporate a coloured stripe sewn onto the clew area as a guide, but although these are quite useful it is sometimes hard to judge when the sheet is exactly in line. Again some sailmakers recommend marking a reference point on the luff and sighting up to this from the sheet fairlead. Both systems are really only applicable to new sails, and even then, because they are only theoretical, leave something to be desired.

The red camber lines in the head and below the sails indicate cross-sections at the top and bottom of each. On the left the sheeting angle is proportionally equal, and the upper and lower black tell-tales (see over), stream aft. The centre sail is sheeted too far forward, and the sail on the right, too far aft.

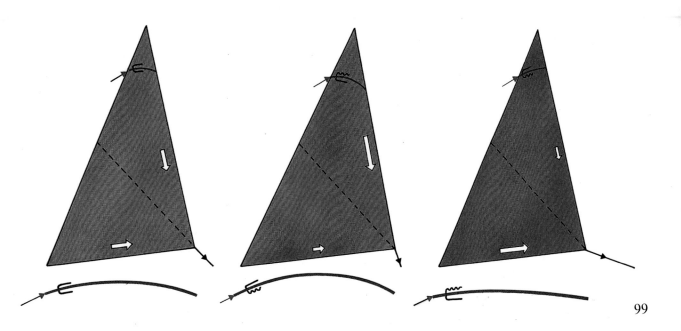

The sail at the top illustrates, in practise, the left hand sail on the previous page. All windward tell-tales are streaming in unison. The centre sail shows the windward tell-tales lifting at the bottom of the sail because the sheet lead is too far forward; and the bottom sail shows the opposite. The sheet lead is now too far aft, and the upper windward tell-tales are lifting.

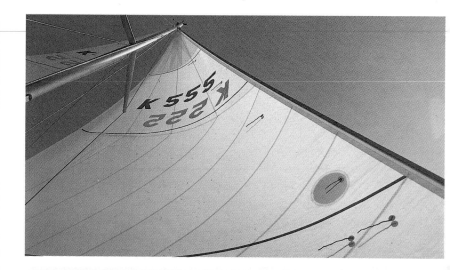

Tell-tales

By far the best system is to fit the luff of the sail with a series of tell-tales. Apart from guaranteeing that the angle of attack is uniformly efficient up and down the entire luff, tell-tales are an invaluable aid to windward helmsmanship.

Tell-tales are short lengths of dark coloured nylon ribbon or wool fixed near to and parallel with the luff of the sail. The exact length of each and the distance they are from the luff, depends on the size of the sail. Consensus indicates 12 to 18 inches aft of the luff for position, and there is little need for them to be longer than 6 inches. It is important that they are free to move in any direction clear of a seam, as there is nothing they enjoy better than sticking like a limpet to the proud stitching.

Whilst stick-on versions are commercially available, by far the easiest and best method is with a darning needle, to pass a length of dark wool through the sail fabric, fixing it in position with an overhand knot on either side. On wet sails wool tails do not seem to stick to the adjacent fabric quite as readily as do the fancier nylon versions.

With the boat on the wind full and by, and the sail sheeted in at a

'guess-it' approximate fairlead position, the windward set of tell-tales should all stream aft. By gently luffing up to windward, some, or all of the tell-tales will lift. If those near the head lift first, the top of the sail is feathering before the lower half. It is rocked too far forward at the head and the fairlead must go forward. Conversely, if those near the bottom lift first the angle of attack of the lower part of the luff is too wide and the fairlead must come aft to narrow it. When all windward tell-tales lift together, then the sheeting angle is correct. Make a note, or actually mark the slider position on the deck. This is the mean position for all further headsail trim.

Further fore and aft adjustment of the headsail sheet lead, along with lateral adjustment, as a means to better meet changing conditions, will be returned to later.

Before leaving basic sheet angles there is one other control which has a direct effect.

Luff Cunningham

Whilst the trend is more and more towards structured fabrics and away from luff tension as a means of controlling maximum depth position, there are many sails which still rely on this method for efficient shape.

Whilst this is commonly achieved via the halyard there are advantages to be gained by using a Cunningham cringle in the luff similar to that used in a mainsail. In all maximum luff headsails a Cunningham allows the sail to be cut with the longest possible luff for lighter airs. Even more important however, a Cunningham allows camber position to be adjusted without the need for also moving the sheet fairlead.

Why, one might ask, is the latter necessary anyway? The answer lies within the leech of the sail. Raising the head, or apex of the triangle, stretches both luff and leech equally. Tension on the bias fabric at the luff draws the maximum depth position forward, but the fill yarns aligned along the leech resist. The result is less twist in the leech; exactly the opposite to what is needed in a strengthening wind.

To free the leech and reintroduce twist aloft, the sheet lead needs to move aft. Tension applied downwards via the Cunningham on the other hand, leaves the head of the sail where it was, and in less structured sails

A simple two-part purchase headsail luff Cunningham, led back to an accessible deck winch.

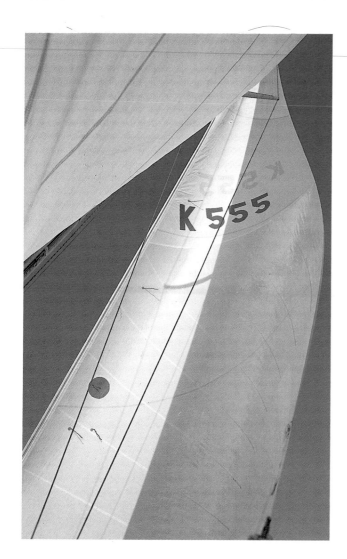

Easing the sheet on a reach (left) has allowed the headsail leech to open, feathering the top. See the upper tell-tale. By moving the sheet lead outboard and forward, the upper sail can be made to work again (right).

will actually open the leech as the effects of tension on the luff work their way aft through the body of the sail.

Sheet tension

Having established a sheeting angle that, when beating to windward, presents the luff at a constant angle of attack to the prevail-

ing flow, is not of course the end of the story. As every sailor knows, control of the headsail to meet changing wind direction and speed also rests with the sheet. As the wind frees so the sheet must be eased to allow the sail to also swivel. Even on the wind, a dying breeze calls for a wider angle of attack in order for flow to be coaxed around the luff and onto the leeward surface.

Unfortunately, easing the sheet immediately upsets the balance of tension within the sail,

and for a very simple reason. Although, at a given tension, the sheet may be exerting the horizontal and vertical components necessary to balance the triangle, the two sides of that triangle are unequal in length. The leech is always longer than the foot, which in practice upsets the whole geometry of the sail every time sheet tension is altered.

Easing the sheet from, for example, close hauled to a close reach, inevitably results in the leech twisting off excessively and he upper area of the luff feathering into the wind.

The same would apply to an even greater degree to the higher aspect mainsail, were it not for the rigid boom. By maintaining a constant downward component, via the vang, the angle of attack of the sail can be controlled as the sail is swivelled around to meet the freeing wind. For a headsail off the wind, compromise becomes the order of the day.

The first move must be to shift the fairlead as far outboard as possible. In this way some downward force component can still be maintained on the leech and upper luff as the whole sail swivels around. A uniform angle of attack is maintained, if only for a very close reach.

Once the wind frees to a reach proper, and the sheet is eased further, twist will once again become excessive and the upper half of the sail will feather.

The only way to reduce it and get the top of the sail working again, is to move the fairlead forward to maintain a degree of vertical control over the leech. This is an unsatisfactory compromise, and it is particularly evident with the fashionable overlapping genoas. Moving the fairlead forward reduces the chord of the sail and dramatically increases camber in the lower sail. Separation and drag inevitably follow; the boat becomes unbalanced and rudder has to be wound on to keep it going in a straight line.

A change hook, on a dedicated reaching sheet, is useful when the lead has to go forward and outboard.

Nevertheless, it is better than sailing with the upper headsail feathered. The amount by which the fairlead should move forward when off the wind will of course vary with each rig, and indeed which size of headsail is up at the time.

The best guides are again the tell-tales. If those aloft are permanently fluttering, move the fairlead forward. If that makes the lower ones dance then try bringing the fairlead a little further aft again. On a reach it is unlikely that they will all stream aft all of the time. Except that is, on very high aspect narrow jibs.

However, as long as sheet tension and the helmsman can keep the mid-luff tell-tales streaming aft constantly, judicial sheet lead positioning should keep all in unison some of the time.

Roller reefing

While most sail development in recent years has been orientated towards higher performance, there is one avenue which

Roller reefing headsails are inclined to 'belly' when shortened in a blow.

has been directed towards greater convenience, and indeed safety.

Today's roller reefing headstay systems stem from an idea for stowing the sail, when not in use, by rolling it up around the forestay. Improvements in materials and design have since made the systems robust enough to withstand the higher torsional loads imposed when the sail is reefed. As sail is shortened the loads running from head and tack back to the clew, move inwards towards the centre of the luff. Compared to the original wire luffs, the alloy foils now incorporated into the systems are better able to cope with these loadings. The systems now allow infinite adjustment of headsail area. However, operation of the systems, and the ability of the foils to cope with the high torsional loads, is greatly enhanced by the presence of an efficient backstay adjuster, capable of combating forestay sag.

Aerodynamically, the presence of the quite substantial luff foil has very little effect, although the increase in weight it adds to the rig must contribute negatively to heeling and pitching moments. Performance is not however the goal. It is the ability to set, trim and restow the headsail, without ever leaving the cockpit, which accounts for their phenomenal popularity.

While a conventional sail will work on a roller reefing system, the best results come from those custom-designed for the purpose. These take account of the two major drawbacks inherent in the systems.

When partially rolled, to cope with higher wind strengths, the built-in camber of a conventional sail will 'belly' in the centre as leech and foot are drawn together. One answer is to start rolling the foil and luff at mid-height, before the tack and head. Some systems provide for this. A better solution appears to be to incorporate a narrow thickening pad within the luff of the sail during manufacture. A tapering strip of expanded-polystyrene, similar to that used for packing fragile items, is sandwiched along the luff to thicken the fabric. Its contribution when rolled around the foil is to flatten the camber in the centre of the sail.

Conventional steel head and tack cringles, with their attendant

104

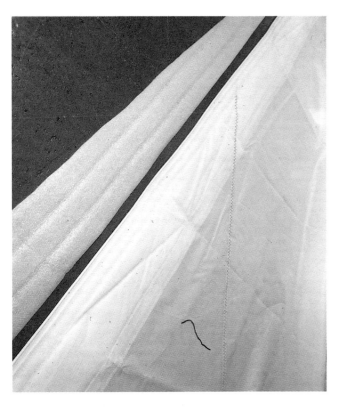

reinforcing patches, also contribute to distortion when the sail is rolled. Tape loops are substituted on the purpose-made sails.

The second drawback is a consequence of the shape of a headsail's plan-form. Ideally the sail should be cut with the clew much higher than normal. The high clew cut, sometimes known as a Yankee, allows the more acutely-angled foot, when rolled, to gradually work up the luff. This more approximates to the manner in which the leech moves down the luff as the sail is rolled up. The result is a much more even, and neater, roll. As well as reducing unnecessary strain on gear and sail fabric, the life expectancy of an evenly rolled sail is increased. Exposure to the ultraviolet rays in sunlight will eventually degrade

Tape loops (below left), in place of bulky metal cringles make for neater rolls at the head and tack. Marks along the foot (below), allow the roller headsail to be shortened by specific amounts.

▼

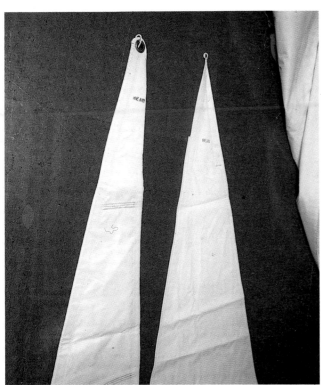

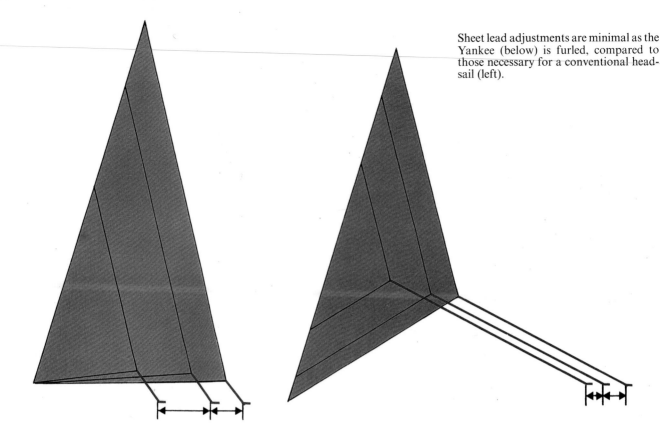

Sheet lead adjustments are minimal as the Yankee (below) is furled, compared to those necessary for a conventional headsail (left).

Dacron. Sails left furled throughout the season are obviously more vulnerable than those stowed below when not in use. To protect those left aloft, coloured strips of acrylic fabric are added along both the foot and the leech. When the sail is rolled up these should effectively shield the Dacron from the harmful rays. Colour is introduced to indicate that the protection is complete, but to some the border effect when the sail is in use is less than aesthetic. A *Dacron* fabric incorporating its own UV protection has been developed, but this is very expensive even when applied just to the leech and foot.

A high-clewed sail will also require less adjustment of the sheet fairlead as the chord is reduced. A true Yankee would require hardly

any adjustment at all, as leech and foot would be almost equal in length, with the sheet lead much further aft than necessary on a conventional headsail. Unfortunately, the height by which the clew can be raised in a cross-cut panel layout is limited by the need to orientate the fill yarns in the same direction as the leech.

The alternative is to use warp-orientated fabric in a simple vertical layout. This allows the sailmaker much greater freedom with which to optimise clew position and foot angle. It also allows heavier cloth to be used for the panels running up and down the leech. The benefit comes when the sail is reefed. The lighter cloth panels, nearer the luff, are safely rolled away and the more substantial panels near the leech are

left to cope with the stronger weather.

Radial constructions take this theme one step further. The panels radiate from the clew, and so the orientation of each remains almost constant throughout the sail whatever the area left unfurled. Panels in the centre of the sail are of lighter fabric than those adjacent to the leech and foot. As the sail is reefed the lighter panels progressively disappear into the luff-roll, until eventually only the heavy panels are left to take the strain.

Heavy weather sailing raises a further issue. As the sail is roller reefed the centre of effort rises. This is the opposite direction to that which it should ideally take. A conventional storm jib is designed and cut to keep the centre

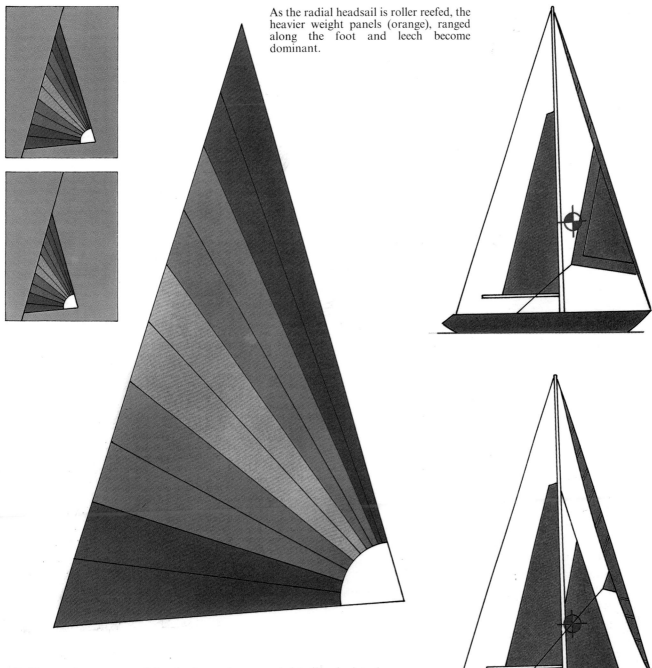

As the radial headsail is roller reefed, the heavier weight panels (orange), ranged along the foot and leech become dominant.

Centre of effort for the top boat is high and forward. Stowing the headsail and substituting a small stormsail on an inner forestay brings the C of E down and back where it belongs.

of effort as low as possible. As is, of course, a storm trysail or deeply reefed mainsail!

Most long distance voyagers agree that the answer is to furl the headsail completely; substituting it, within the fore-triangle, with a heavyweight jib hoisted on an inner forestay. In other words a storm staysail. This will lower the centre of effort, and also bring it aft; concentrating that of both headsail and mainsail close to the boat's centre of lateral balance.

Tuning the rig

Tuning the rig is a somewhat romantic phrase, conjuring thoughts more musical than nautical. In practice it is almost totally mechanical.

The sailmaker, it will be remembered, has striven to turn a moulded sail shape into one which will fly effectively. That flying shape will in the end rely on the efficient support of the rig upon which it is hung.

As important in seamanship terms is the need to maintain the geometrical equation within which the mast and stays of the rig were designed. In other words a badly set-up rig will not be as strong as it was designed to be.

For the racing sailor there is a further consideration. The rig, and tensions within, provide him with a measure of control over shape within the sail. The set of a performance rig must therefore include a measure of adjustability with which the sail trimmer can play.

Tuning is nothing to do with plucking a taut wire stay and listening to the note of vibration. Leave that to the piano tuner and his fork. Tuning, or setting up, the rig is all about achieving the correct geometry and tensions for the mast and its supporting stays.

Neither is rig tuning the sole province of the performance sailor. To have read this far displays more than enough interest in sail efficiency to justify the few hours needed to properly set up the rig of even the most committed cruiser. The rewards from basic tuning are available to all, and at their simplest, on the one hand will provide a framework in which the sails will work as they were designed; and on the other give the sailor basic confidence in the integrity of the rig.

Addressing first the fundamentals, both masthead and fractional rigs can be combined. Later, the more refined techniques necessary to allow adjustment factors for each will be dealt with.

Lateral mast bend

The primary objective on any displacement boat is to reduce any sideways bend in the mast between the deck and the point aloft where the cap shrouds meet. On a masthead rigged boat this is at the top of the spar; whilst on a fractional rig it is usually at the level where the forestay meets the mast.

In both cases the aim is to laterally position that point directly above the keel, or deck partner, and keep it there whatever the wind strength. At the same time the mast has to be, in a lateral plane, as straight as possible. Were it to bow out under compression to either side, then the distance between masthead and deck would be reduced, and the forestay would sag off to leeward. In such circumstances no amount of extra tension via the backstay will straighten out the forestay, and as the wind increases the mast will simply bow more acutely. This is exactly the opposite to what is needed to maintain efficient sail shape, and will eventually compromise the integrity of the spar. This is particularly true if the bow in the mast is to windward. As the mast head moves to leeward, so the angle made between the cap shroud and the spar is reduced. Maintenance of the design angles made between the shrouds, and both spreaders and the spar, is a fundamental in the designed strength of the rig.

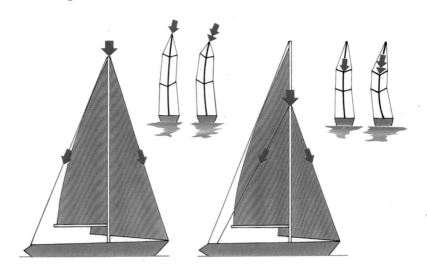

Tensions in the fore and backstays combine to compress the mast downwards (red arrows). Any lateral bend will increase as more load is exerted.

Photo: Barry Pickthall

Masthead to deck edge measurements are taken on both sides of the spar using a non-stretching (metal) tape.

Both from the efficiency and safety viewpoints therefore, a laterally straight and rigid spar is essential. How then is this to be achieved?

For many, setting up the mast is a job left to the shipyard when the boat is launched each season. The quite reasonable argument is that their riggers have much more experience in setting up the tensions than could ever be accumulated by the recreational sailor. The drawback is that however experienced they may be, the job will be done at the dockside, when ideally it should be tackled both there and out on the water with the sails hoisted.

The procedure is easily understood and well within the competence of any sailor.

At the dockside

The first task is to laterally centre the point where the cap shrouds join the mast. Start with all rigging loose and, if the spar is keel stepped, all wedges removed from around the partners.

Now hoist a steel tape measure on the main halyard, or in the case of a fractional-rig, a genoa halyard, and measure the distances from the exit sheave to exactly the same points on either side of the deck edge. Any discrepancy between the two measu-

The one-in-sixty rule. For each degree of rake, mast height (H) divided by sixty, gives one unit of distance (D), aft of the spar at deck level. ▼

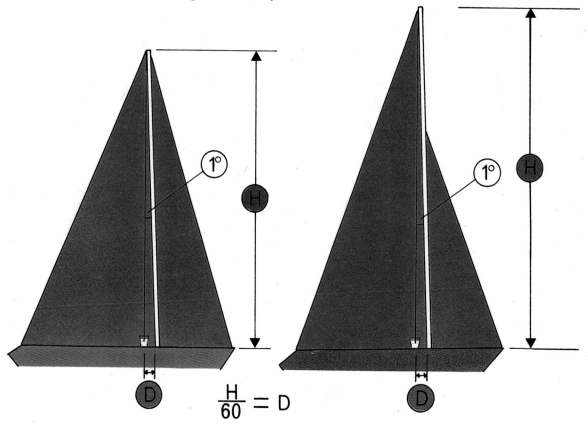

$$\frac{H}{60} = D$$

ements can be eliminated by adjustment of the cap-shroud bottle screws (turnbuckles). It is all too easy to keep increasing tension whilst getting the masthead centred. If one side needs tightening down, unscrew the opposite by a similar number of turns to allow the head to move. Lower and intermediate shrouds should be very loose whilst this is being done.

Once the mast is centred athwartships and the cap shrouds on either side are hand tight, attention can be turned to positioning it fore and aft.

Fore and aft

The difference here is that whilst lateral bend has to be permanently eliminated, a degree of fore and aft bend in the main spar, particularly if it can be adjusted while sailing, is a definite benefit. Consequently, fine tuning in the fore and aft plane can only be achieved whilst actually sailing.

What can be determined at the dockside is the degree of rake, and if desired, pre-bend. This is particularly relevant to masthead rigged boats upon which backstay adjustment whilst sailing is not envisaged. For them this position will be permanent, but even for more sophisticated adjustable rigs, it is a predetermined position of some importance.

On all boats, therefore, the first step is to establish a straight fore and aft mast with around 1 degree of rake. For those with adjustable or running backstays, which include most fractional rigged boats, this position will equate with that for sailing down wind. That is with the mast straight, giving the greatest depth of camber possible to the mainsail.

Remember, at this stage, the aim is to position the apex of the triangular forces acting on the spar. For all practical purposes, this position is best found using the main halyard as a plumb line and shackling a fairly heavy weight to its end. Any excess swing in this makeshift plumb can be damped out by letting the weight dangle in a bucket of water resting on deck. The boom is best removed and laid aside, but this is not vital.

One degree of rake on a 30 foot spar equates to some 6 inches at the foot of the mast between its aft edge and the plumb. For a 60 foot tall spar the distance is 12 inches, and pro rata.

With the correct rake established, the forestay and backstay of a masthead boat can be made up hand tight—a tension similar to that of the cap shrouds. The forestay and backstay on a fractional rig can now be made up just hand tight to keep the mast straight. Any further tensioning of the forestay will be achieved by tightening the runners or in the case of aft-swept spreader rigs, the shrouds, about which more later.

A keel-stepped mast should, at this stage, be in contact with the aft edge of the partner hole in the deck. If it is not, and the heel can be adjusted, it is worth moving this aft until it does.

Backstay adjusters range from a simple cam-lever to powerful hydraulic pumps.

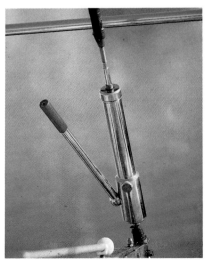

For a rig which will not be adjusted whilst sailing the measurement process ends here. Both fore and backstay on a masthead rig can be hardened down by equal amounts as described a little later. However, more and more masthead boats are being equipped with the means with which to adjust the backstay and so control sail shape. These range from sophisticated hydraulic rams, through wheel devices, down to simple, but highly effective and very inexpensive pulley systems. As the efficient trim of modern headsails and mainsails depend more and more on rig adjustment, a system is well worth incorporating. For roller-reefing headsails, as was mentioned, an adjustable backstay plays a vital role.

Returning to the rig-tuning process however, the presence of a system for backstay adjustment calls for further games with the plumb and bucket of water. Leaving the forestay hand tight, the backstay or runners (in the case of a fractional rig), should now be tightened down hard until the mast is raked aft by some 3 degrees. Using the same 1 in 60 rule this equates to around 3 feet on a 60 foot spar and about 1.5 feet on one 30 feet high. In practice forestay tension should now approximate to that needed when sailing to windward. However, this will depend in some measure on the reader's understanding of 'hand tight', and the forestay may need a degree of further hardening down.

Achieving a straight forestay on fractional rig boats is dependent on the effectiveness of its running backstay system.

The aim must be to keep the apex of the triangle in the same fore and aft plane. Both forestay and backstay must therefore be tensioned by equal amounts. In effect, the tuner is establishing the working length of the forestay.

If a gauge is incorporated in the backstay adjustment device a good load limit for fore/backstay tension is one third of the safe working load of the wire or rod. Without a gauge, the tensioning down on the forestay bottle screw—in step with an equal amount on the adjustable backstay—can be as hard as an average size man can achieve using a large (18 inch) screwdriver and a similar length adjustable wrench. Enthusiasm should always be tempered, however, by the condition of rig and vessel.

To achieve the same end within a fractional rig, for backstay read running backstays. Once sailing, the permanent (masthead) backstay will be under constant adjustment controlling the depth-to-chord ratio and twist of the mainsail. At this stage, having already adjusted it to approximately that for a straight mast, it can be safely ignored until a mainsail is hoisted.

Before going sailing just three jobs remain. The mast, if keel-stepped, must be secured firmly at the partners; the cap shrouds have to be tightened down hard an equal number of turns on either side; and any slack should be taken out of the lower and, if fitted, intermediary shrouds. For the latter no great precision is necessary. Their turn will come

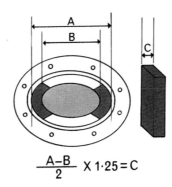
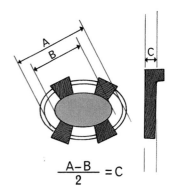

$$\frac{A-B}{2} \times 1{\cdot}25 = C$$

$$\frac{A-B}{2} = C$$

Rubber wedges (left) are relatively thicker than wooden chocks (right) for the space between spar and partner.

In place, rubber wedges are a really tight fit. ▼

once the sails are hoisted and the boat put on the wind.

The tension for the cap shrouds is very tight. So tight that once on the wind, there will be negligible slack in the one to leeward. Again, the best an average man can achieve with an 18 inch set of tools will do for the time being.

Wedging

Wedging the spar in the partners is worthy of a little more at-tention. It is extremely important both from the viewpoint of safety and confidence in the rig, and that of control. Yet many new boats are delivered from their builders without any provision for chocking the mast—let alone the chocks being in place. Likewise, unless asked, few boatyards will install chocks where previously there were none.

The best are made from very high grade Naval or pure tan gum rubber slabs slightly deeper than the partner hole; and with a combined thickness of 1.25 times the space left between the mast and the partner wall. Because of the difficulty encountered in inserting such wedges, wooden pegs are commonly substituted. These are much more easily driven in around the mast and as long as they are periodically inspected—for possible splitting—are normally satisfactory.

The aim must be to chock the mast firmly into the centre of the hole, eliminating any fore and aft movement and severely restricting any from side to side. Centering a mast which was in contact with the aft edge of the partners achieves a slight bowing effect as the spar is forced forward in relation to its heel. This pre-bend, or set, in fact makes it more rigid.

The boat is now ready to go sailing.

On the water

Ideal conditions are those in which, with a foresail and full mainsail hoisted, the boat will heel between 20 and 25 degrees. The adjustable backstay, or runners, should be tensioned to provide a tight forestay. First check for slackness in the leeward cap shroud. It should look straight and any sign of floppiness will have to be taken out. First take up a turn or two on the leeward bottle screw, then tack and take

Lateral mast bend is obvious to an eye placed close to the mainsail track. On the left, the mast is bowing to windward in the middle; on the right, it is sagging above the lower spreader.

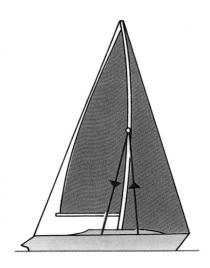
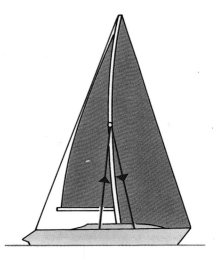

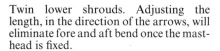
Twin lower shrouds. Adjusting the length, in the direction of the arrows, will eliminate fore and aft bend once the masthead is fixed.

up exactly the same amount on the other side. Remember the leeward cap on either tack should not be tight—just not floppy slack.

Now place one eye as close as possible to the mainsail groove. By looking aloft, it will become very clear if any athwartship bend is developing between eye level and where the cap shrouds meet.

If the centre of the mast sags away to leeward, tighten down on the windward lower shroud(s) until the spar straightens out. If the mid section is bowing to windward slacken the windward shroud(s) until the same effect has been achieved. Then tack the boat and do exactly the same on the other side. In practice the easiest way by far is to tack the boat after each sighting, adjusting the then leeward and slacker shroud by half or one complete turn. Then check the effect of the new tension in the windward shroud, which

was adjusted whilst on the previous tack.

Masts with more than single spreaders could naturally develop a combination of sag and bow to windward dependent on the relative tension of upper, intermediate or lower shrouds. In this case each must be balanced working from the top downwards, so that at each spreader root and where cap shrouds join the mast, are all in a straight line.

However many spreaders are fitted one rule remains. Under no circumstances, whatever bend characteristics the mast might exhibit, make any further adjustments to either cap shroud.

Twin lower shrouds

Whilst no longer the fashion, many boats retain a rig with twin lower shrouds. In following the above procedure, both fore and aft lower shrouds have to be adjusted an equal amount on either tack. However, once the mast is straight athwartships there is a further step. Viewing the mast from the side, check that the pre-

bend, or set, is still there. An excessive amount of bend can be counteracted by loosening, half a turn at a time, the forward bottlescrew, and tightening down, by an equal amount on the after.

Potentially far more critical is a mast bowing aft. Correction, which is vital, calls for the reverse of the above. Take down on the forward shroud whilst loosening the after. As before, tack and carry out the same job on the other side. On a deck-stepped mast this may be the only means of inducing a little pre-bend, or set, into the spar.

Baby/inner forestay

The first element to disappear along the road towards the all-singing, all-dancing infinitely adjustable rig, was the forward lower shroud. The element of athwartship support it gave was delegated to its after twin, and both forward shrouds were consolidated into a single inner forestay. The implications for mast tuning are essentially simplified. Once lateral bend is eliminated with the aft lower shrouds, the inner or baby stay can be tensioned to maintain the pre-bend, or set, in the spar, countering the backward force from the lower shrouds.

With improvement in sail cloth structures came the need to control mainsail shape by inducing further bend into the mast whilst sailing. The means were already to hand. By increasing tension of the inner forestay the mast would bow forward, provided it was not restrained by the aft lower shrouds.

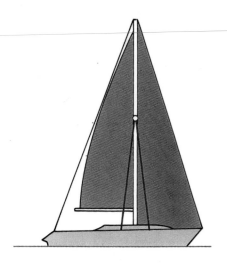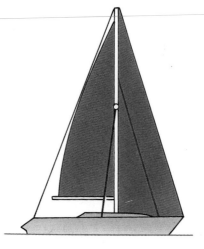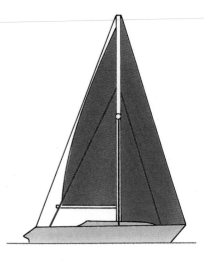

The popularity of twin lowers (left) has waned in favour of an inner forestay and running backstays (blue). Lower shrouds (red), in the same plane as the mast, allow the spar to be bent as an aid to sail trim.

The answer was to move the lowers into the same plane as the mast and its cap shrouds. Now mast bend could be easily and quickly induced. However, with no counterbalance, the amount of bend induced required caution. With only the integral stiffness of the spar itself to counter babystay tension, enthusiasm for the latter was wisely tempered.

Enter, or to be strictly accurate, re-enter the running backstay. Ironically, this more tangible check on mast bend actually encouraged it. Just as on the fractional rig where the amount of forestay sag and headsail camber could be accurately controlled by a running backstay, so on a masthead rig, the same element working against an inner forestay could control precisely the mast bend and consequent depth-to-chord ratio of the mainsail.

Whilst on the subject of inner forestays, a word about their relevance to the more cruising orientated sailor. A babystay, where fitted to a cruising spar, usually plays a more temporary role. In heavier weather it inhibits 'panting' in the mast, particularly when counterbalanced by a running backstay. However in lighter airs, any benefit is more than outweighed by its obstructive quality—strung right across the path of a tacking headsail. For the cruiser then, the need to include this type of inner/baby forestay in the rig tuning sequence is unnecessary. For the performance sailor it is a constantly adjustable feast as will be seen.

Forestay sag

Whilst still afloat, one of the two fundamentals which need to be sorted out is the maximum forestay tension. Forestay tension is controlled on a masthead boat by backstay tension; and in a fractional rig by running backstay tension. A very small number of specialised racing boats have ad-

justable forestays but they are of no relevance here.

Tension on the fore and backstay was wound on, it will be recalled, before the boat left the dock. It is now time to check that the two are sufficiently tight.

First make sure the tension on the backstay is recorded, either with a measure from a fixed point on the boat, or with a piece of tape around the thread of the bottle screw. With the boat on the wind and heeled between 20 and 25 degrees, the backstay can now be slackened an inch or so.

With a helper looking up the forestay, begin to wind the backstay back down again. The effect on the forestay will be a proportional reduction in sag. However as the backstay continues to be wound down, this forestay effect will diminish and then disappear altogether. Further tension on the backstay would now be counterproductive. Either the boat will bend like a banana, or the mast will punch a hole in its bottom.

The point when backstay tension no longer reduces headsail

This simple system allows the inner fore-stay to be neatly stowed, out of the fore-triangle, in lighter weather. ▶

sag should be calibrated. On the non-adjustable rig, provided the boat is in sound condition, it could well be the tension for all season. However, any great discrepancy between this maximum tension and that originally wound in at the dockside may mean some counter adjustment in the forestay itself. This is in order that the correct mast rake is maintained.

Before leaving forestay sag, a word on two of the differences between rod and 1 × 19 wire for standing rigging.

Size for size, the wisdom goes, rod is stronger than wire rope. In fact, as they are both the same material, size for size they are the same strength. Where they do differ is in their stretch characteristics. Under an increasing load rod reaches its maximum extension more quickly and with far less elongation, than does wire. Rod on the other hand is much more expensive, is less user friendly and is prone to damage.

Whichever is used, under tension it will stretch to some degree during a typical six month season. It is well worth, once or twice each season, checking lateral bend in the mast as previously described. The longer cap shrouds will naturally stretch more than

Tape around the threaded part of this adjustable backstay wheel marks the maximum tension point when the backstay is loaded down. ▼

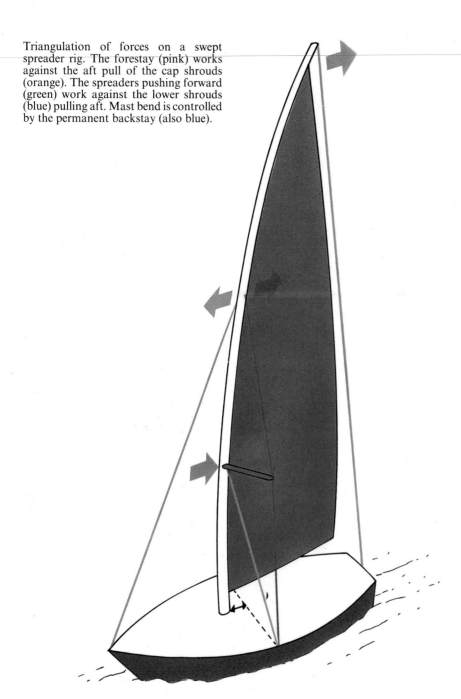

Triangulation of forces on a swept spreader rig. The forestay (pink) works against the aft pull of the cap shrouds (orange). The spreaders pushing forward (green) work against the lower shrouds (blue) pulling aft. Mast bend is controlled by the permanent backstay (also blue).

without the means of forestay/backstay adjustment while sailing, the mast is also now fixed at an optimum point and tension for upwind sailing.

Further, for those masthead rigged boats with a device for adjusting forestay/backstay tension, the range, or limits, of adjustment have been established. For windward work maximum tension to minimise forestay sag has been found and noted, as has minimum backstay tension to allow the mast to straighten and the forestay to sag; both desirable down wind.

Equally, for fractional-rigged boats the same range or limits have been achieved using the running backstays to tension the shorter forestay.

The only variable factors remaining are the standing backstay on a fractional rig, and those controls on a sophisticated masthead rig relating also to mainsail shape. Both control mast bend as a means of adjusting the depth-to-chord ratio within the mainsail. This will be dealt with in the section on sail trim.

Swept spreaders

There is however one popular rig about which very little of the aforementioned applies. This is the fractional mast which depends for both athwartship and fore and aft support on a single pair of aft-swept spreaders forming a tension-lock between the shrouds and forestay. Although this rig allows rather more forestay sag than might be wished, it is popular on smaller boats because the need for running backstays is

the lowers and intermediates, and may need to be tightened down a turn or two. Remember, however, to tighten both by precisely the same amount.

To recap then. The mast for both a fractional or masthead rig is now correctly positioned and tensioned in the athwartship plane. For a simple masthead rig, dispensed with.

Both cap and lower shrouds lead from chainplates aft of the mast. As well as athwartship support, the lowers provide an aft force at spreader level, against the forward push provided by the cap shrouds working through the aft-swept spreaders. This locking tension provides support for the rig downwind. It also counters sag in the forestay at the point where the cap shrouds meet the mast.

The tuning process therefore depends for its success on maximising the locking effect. The first step is to securely chock the mast in the partners with rather more pre-bend than for a more conventional rig.

Using a tape measure from the masthead, as described earlier, centre the mast athwartships, and leave the cap shrouds hand tight. Once sailing with the boat on the wind and heeled between 20 and 25 degrees, tighten down the permanent backstay until a diagonal crease appears in the mainsail running from the clew to mid luff. When increased luff tension via the Cunningham fails to eliminate this crease the mast is at maximum useful bend. One word of caution however. For any fractional or ultra-bendy rig it is worth establishing with the mast-maker the maximum bend of the spar itself. It is unlikely, but possible, that the sail has been cut too full for the spar in question, in which case the above technique will induce too much bend with

disastrous consequences.

Maximum mast bend on this rig will release tension on the cap shroud which can now be hand tightened again an equal amount

either side. Sighting up the main track, any sag or bow in the spar at the spreaders can be eliminated on either tack by adjusting the lower shrouds, leaving them just

Excessive mast bend will cause diagonal creases to form from the clew up into the luff of the mainsail.

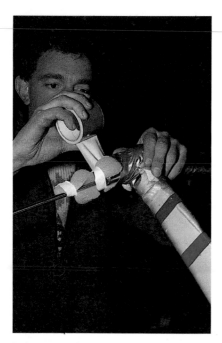

Polystyrene foam, bound tightly with sticky tape, makes an effective, and cheap, pad around spreader ends. The red and blue tape bands give the headsail trimmer a reference for the leech distance off the spreader once sailing.

hand tight on both sides.

Once the permanent backstay is released and the mast straightened again, considerable tension between the shrouds, spreaders and forestay will effectively lock the rig in place. The spar itself will exhibit substantial pre-bend, or set, reducing headstay sag and athwartship bend as far as is possible with this type of rig.

Taping up

In 99 cases out of 100 the foregoing techniques are the frameworks within which the rigs of all displacement boats can be effectively tuned.

Returning to the dock, all standing rigging bottle screws can

120

be locked, and then taped-up with PVC waterproof tape. Split-pins (cotter pins) for shroud bottle screws should be inserted from outboard inwards and then heavily taped over. Special non-sticky rigging tape which welds to itself when stretched is popular. It lasts longer in sunlight and is very easy to cut away at the end of the season. However, the price is astronomic.

Whilst on the subject of taping, spreader ends are a notorious ripper of sails, as are steaming lights, spinnaker pole cups and other protrusions on the foreside of the mast. All sharp edges must be either taped, filed off, or faired with a blob of silicone sealer. Headsails particularly, have an extraordinary ability to seek out and ravage themselves on any sharp point left uncovered.

Rake and helm

The fly in the ointment to all mast tuning has been left until the end, largely for fear of putting readers off tackling the job for themselves. In some cases, it has to be said, the degree of mast-rake recommended earlier will have a detrimental effect on the helm of a particular boat. Equally it has to be said that most architects will draw the rig using much the same rake as described.

It is anyway worth understanding the effect of rake on the helm.

Increasing rake, that is moving the whole rig aft, also moves aft the centre of effort of the sails in relation to the centre of resistance of the hull. To balance

this rudder has to be introduced to counteract the boat swinging into the wind. Raking the mast aft therefore increases weather helm. The reverse is also true. Moving the mast and rig forward reduces weather helm and will eventually result in lee helm.

All sailors know that a modicum, say 5 degrees, of weather helm provides 'feel' when beating to windward.

If, after the tuning sail, a boat displays either too much, or too little weather helm then further adjustments of the forestay will be necessary. Only on a masthead yacht with no device for backstay adjustment will it be necessary to also alter the backstay; although the calibrations for maximum and minimum backstay tensions will have to be reviewed.

A Swedish fid is used to put a calibration whipping through the lay of a wire halyard.

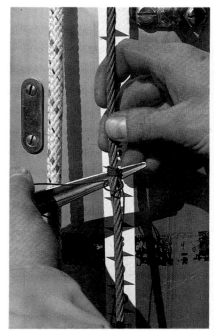

around the world ever need reminding to leave forestay length well alone when de-rigging and unstepping a mast.

Running rigging

Turning to running rigging, all halyards will benefit from being calibrated to work within the newly tuned rig. Calibration, de rigueur for the racing fraternity, is arguably equally important on a conservative cruiser. With the universal advent of stretchy tape luffs, it is efficient to know minimum hoist and vital to know maximum hoist.

Calibration means marking the halyard so that it can be lined up with a series of static reference points, either on the mast or on deck, when a particular tension is desired. Most sailmakers produce strips of calibrated self-adhesive plastic to aid this.

On any halyard, marks made with sticky tape, or even whippings, are of little use. They soon move or wear as the halyard passes through blocks or over sheaves.

For wire halyards, the best way is to open the lay with a fid and tie a whipping twine seizing actually through the wire. An even more permanent mark can be made by tying seizing wire through the lay, but the advantages are more than outweighed by the risk to cut fingers and thumbs.

Incidentally, fingers and thumbs also benefit greatly if the halyards are made from galvanised wire in preference to the smarter stainless steel variety. The

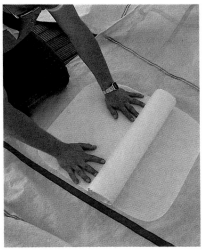

Laminate sails need leech patches for protection from spreader ends. Exact positions can only be marked when the sail is hoisted and sheeted in (top). The patches (left) are made from sticky-backed *Dacron*, similar to that used for sail numbers and insignia.

Forestay length and rake should be a once and for all exercise. There is no reason why the forestay bottle screw need be altered again, once the sailor is comfortable with the feel of the helm. Indeed few boatyard riggers

121

latter is prone to work hardening. As it becomes brittle so individual strands break. Stainless foresail halyards are particularly susceptible to failing in the area adjacent to the shackle, where, when hoisted, the wire is bent over the masthead sheave. The resulting 'needles' can wreak painful havoc with fingers when shackling the halyard to the head of the sail prior to hoisting.

For mainsail halyards, wire is in any case being rapidly dis-placed by the new *Kevlar* cored ropes. The stretched character-istics of these new ropes are only slightly greater than those of wire. For mainsail halyards where loads are much less than for head-sails, the handling advantages more than compensate for the relatively higher stretch.

The tension reference mark on these, and conventional rope halyards can be made by sewing a twine whipping through the lay with a palm and needle.

Wire strops (blue), added to the head of smaller foresails, allow one set of halyard calibration marks to serve for all.

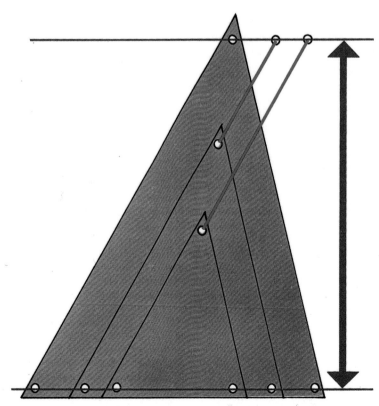

Foresail halyards

The calibration necessary for a headsail halyard will depend on the fabric from which the sails are made. Standard *Dacron* sails re-quire greater luff adjustments to maintain shape, than for example the increasingly popular lamin-ates. Indeed, as laminating tech-niques progress, little or no luff adjustment is the eventual goal.

However, in all cases it is worth determining, and marking, the position of maximum hoist for the halyard. The primary purpose here is to avoid pulling the halyard shackle splice into the masthead sheave. Under load, damage to either or both is inevitable.

This is a job best done at the dockside. Hoist a sheet or similar length of line on the halyard until the splice runs into the masthead sheave. Erring on the side of cau-tion, the tail of the halyard can now be marked, as previously de-scribed, an inch or two past the reference point made on either the mast or deck. If calibration strips are used, this will be past the high-est number. Under tension, with a sail hoisted, the stretch in the halyard will maintain the neces-sary clearance between shackle splice and sheave.

This then becomes a reference point beyond which the halyard must not be tensioned, whatever sail is hoisted. If the sailmaker has done his job correctly, it should also approximate to the hoist for a full size *Dacron* headsail trimmed for the top of its wind range. If not, and this can only be judged

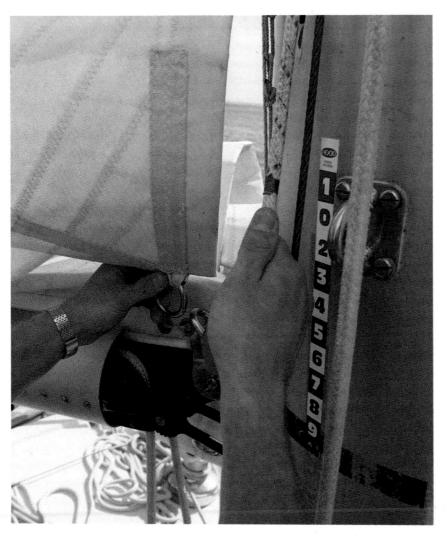

The mark on this *Kevlar* main halyard registers the amount it has to be eased when reefing, in order for the luff cringle to be slipped onto the gooseneck hook.

by sailing in those conditions, with maximum camber correctly positioned, a further note must be made of where the halyard mark is in relation to the calibration on mast or deck.

For full size headsails made from more structured *Dacron* and laminates a more cautious approach is recommended. Over-stretching the luff of such fabrics can cause permanent distortion. They should first be hoisted until the wrinkles in the luff disappear. Any further tension to position maximum camber can then be gradually increased, a little at a time. The range of halyard travel to maximum hoist will be a fraction of that for a conventional *Dacron* sail.

Minimum hoist for the full size headsail is also worth noting. For the racing sailor this will be particularly useful as a guide to tension when hoisting a headsail in light conditions.

So far of course these halyard positions only relate to maximum size sails, or at least, to the biggest headsail carried on board the boat. What then about smaller headsails when the time comes to change down a size?

The best answer is to have the sailmaker add a wire strop to the head of each; in effect extending the luff lengths so that all are exactly the same as that of the largest headsail. In this way the position of maximum hoist for the largest applies equally throughout the headsail inventory.

Mainsail halyards

The more universal adoption of luff Cunninghams with the modern mainsail simplifies calibration of the halyard.

With the sail hoisted to its limit, invariably marked with a black band around the masthead, the halyard can be marked relative to a point on the lower mast or deck. This obviates the need to judge the relationship of the headboard to the black band every time the sail is hoisted.

It is also worth marking the main halyard at those points where it is necessary to slack off when taking in a slab reef. The mainsail halyard can then be dumped to those marks, allowing the reef tack to be slipped onto the gooseneck hook. This technique originated on the race course, but is potentially of even greater usefulness to the shorthanded cruiser.

Trim

In previous pages the thrust has been on the nature of sails, how they work, and the degree of control over them available to the sailor. If that was the courtship, effective sail trim can be said to represent the marriage leading to a happy life thereafter.

At the front of the racing fleet, trim is a paramount factor, calling for constant and absolute devotion. At this level it is a full time, never-ending round of action, balancing sails and rig against the wind. Unfortunately a great deal that is written on the subject attempts to document this level of activity and expertise; in many cases confusing and frustrating those with a more level-headed interest. Much also reflects a personal technique which ignores, and sometimes even contradicts, the basics.

The basics are relatively simple. It is perhaps worth a short recap, with the question, what is sail trim trying to achieve?

Sails produce motive power for the boat but in the process also produce drag. The forward drive results from the interaction of forces between the sails and the boat, and in particular its keel and underwater area.

The aim of sail trim must therefore be to maximise lift and minimise drag, but also to maintain a balance between the forces working both above and below the water.

Balance

In an ideal beat to windward the total side force generated by the sails will be equal and opposite to the combined lateral resistance of keel and rudder. Forward drive is then a product of lift from the sails and drag from sails and the underwater body of the boat.

However, any lateral imbalance of the forces within the total rig will cause an equal and opposite change in the boat's direction of travel.

In the top picture, the upper finger represents the centre of underwater resistance, and the two lower ones the sideways component generated by foresail and mainsail. Any increase in the component of one sail over the other, will cause the pencil boat to swivel on its underwater axis. With increased mainsail force the boat heads up to windward (middle picture).

To keep the boat tracking in a straight line, rudder has to be applied as the counterbalance, (bottom picture) with a resultant increase in drag.

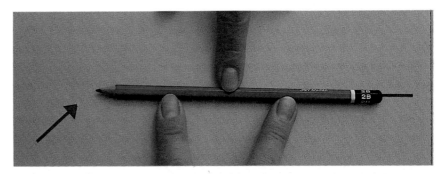

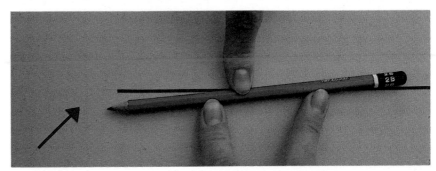

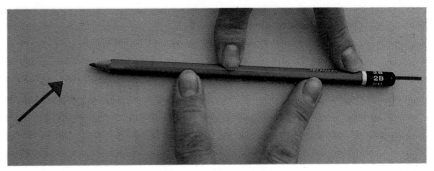

Photo: Rick Tomlinson/PPL

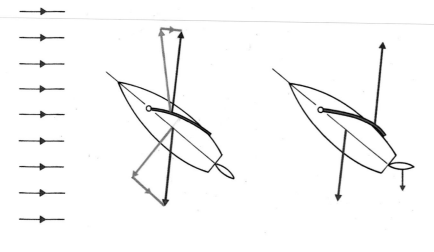

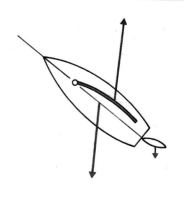

A badly shaped sail (centre), or one sheeted too close to the centreline (right), moves the total sail force (red) in relation to that generated by the keel (blue). As the centre of sail effort moves aft, so rudder and drag have to be introduced to keep the boat tracking in a straight line.

Assuming the mast is correctly raked, imbalance of the rig can happen in two ways: the first is when a disproportionate amount of sideways force is generated in either sail; the second is when the plane made by both sails is incorrectly angled to the centre line.

The first is a product of individual sail shape. It is worth noting that a badly trimmed foresail also has a significant effect on balance, even though it is further forward than the main. A foresail with the draft aft unbalances the designed lift to drag ratio upon which the whole sail plan has been drawn.

The second is the result of trimming the entire aerofoil section incorrectly. As it forms the trailing edge of the rig, the mainsail plays the predominant role in this type of unbalanced trim.

Lift v drag

The other target for sail trim is to maximise lift and reduce drag and so move the total force generated as far forward as possible in line with the direction of travel.

At its simplest this means shaping the foresail for maximum lift. Working as it does in apparent wind freed by the circular flow of the mainsail, this sail is anyway angled further across the wind. However, that very same circular flow depends equally for its energy on both correct mainsail trim and a successful marriage between both sails. Here, it is worth noting that this interrelationship governs successful circular flow around a narrow jib just as much as it does for a large overlapping genoa. The gap between the two may be much wider, but the effect each sail has on its partner is similar. Circular

flow and the benefits it brings, still exist.

Aerodynamically, therefore, the sails must work as one, and the total aerofoil must be trimmed to the correct angle with the centreline of the boat.

As the sails are working as one, this is often viewed as trimming the luff of the headsail and the leech of the main. Using that as a starting point, the areas where they interact closely can for the moment be left to one side.

Mainsail leech trim

As was noted above, the mainsail, and particularly its leech area, has a significant effect on boat balance. This must be the initial consideration. The angle the mainsail makes with the centreline and with accelerated apparent wind flow is controlled by the sheet. The luff area is a poor indication of angle of attack due to the separated flow caused by the mast. Equally, main sheet tension also governs the degree of twist in the leech of the sail. What is needed is an indication that flow is moving smoothly off the trailing edge of the sail, and that this is happening over its entire height.

Leech tell-tales

One method is to sew nylon or wool tell-tales to the aft end of each batten pocket. Whilst these are streaming aft of the leech, the sail is flat enough, with sufficient twist to allow flow to exit efficiently. However, the sail may be too flat or have too much twist to generate maximum power in the prevailing conditions.

Normally too great a camber, or too much twist will make the tell-tales first flutter upwards and then flatten back along the lee side of the sail.

Optimum twist and camber is when the tell-tales, particularly those adjacent to the upper battens, lift about half of the time.

The leech tell-tale at the top batten pocket will be the first to stop streaming aft (left), and disappear behind the lee of the sail (right).

Top batten

Another method, less time absorbing and certainly easier on the neck, is to use the designer's original skill to maintain the correct twist originally built into the sail.

In ninety cases out of one hundred, the correct amount of twist for any but the very lightest of airs will be when the top batten is parallel with the boom. To sight this accurately calls for one eye underneath the boom while one hand trims the mainsheet.

Naturally, having first sheeted the mainsail to neutralise any im-

balance on the helm, any adjustment in twist with the sheet will have a knock-on effect. This is where an athwartship traveller plays such an important role. Twist control then becomes the sole province of the sheet, and the angle between sail and centreline can be adjusted by moving the traveller.

Twist control also affects both chord-to-depth ratio aloft and the position of maximum draft. However, as long as either the tell-tales are flying or the top batten parallels the boom, this for the moment can be ignored and attention turned to the leading edge of the aerofoil at the luff of the headsail.

Headsail luff trim

As the leading edge of the rig, the shape of the headsail luff and the angle of attack at which it is presented to prevailing air flow governs all that follows.

In particular it dictates the angle at which the boat can be pointed into the wind. Whilst as a result of trim, it is the sail that alters its angle of attack to the wind, it is sometimes easier to think of this remaining constant and the boat altering direction beneath it.

Take for instance the basic trim afforded by the sheet. As the wind decreases, it will no longer bend around the sharp luff of a tightly sheeted headsail. To reduce the separation bubble and reattach flow, the sheet must be eased, making the luff angle smaller. Unless the boat also points lower however, the sail will then luff. It is actually the boat angle which has changed. This is admittedly a simplification, but one worth taking on board.

In the previous section the correct positioning of the sheet lead angle was described. With all luff tell-tales acting in unison the sail could be said to be meeting the oncoming flow up and down the luff at a uniform angle of attack.

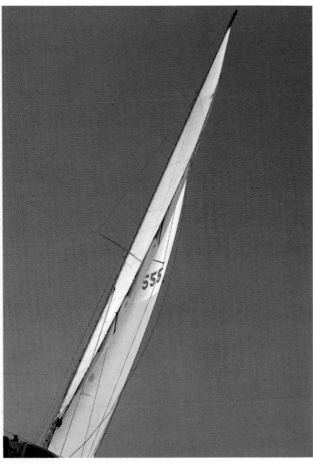

Sighting up from below the boom, the top batten (bottom left) reveals a tight leech. In the centre pair of pictures, the batten falls off to leeward, reflecting too much twist. On the right, the batten parallel to the boom is a good indication of correct leech trim.

129

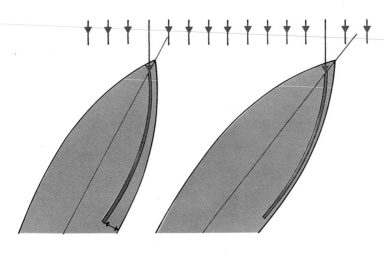

Sheeting inboard (left) allows a finer angle of attack. The boat can point higher than when the sheet lead is outboard (right).

◄

At its most basic, this combined with the correct positioning of maximum depth of camber could be described as adequate headsail trim. This latter, as has also been described, is a function of luff tension balancing that from the sheet. However there are re-

The distance between leech and top spreader is a good indication of headsail twist (left). In the centre, the sheet lead is too far forward, reducing twist; and on the right, is too far aft, freeing the leech. ▼

finements, which although still simple, will increase the sail's effectiveness.

Lead angle

Altering the athwartship position of the headsail sheet lead changes the angle of attack of the luff, but also has a side effect on the depth-to-chord ratio throughout the sail.

Narrowing the lead angle—that is moving the fairlead inboard—allows the boat to swivel up in relation to the angle the sail makes with the wind. In other words the boat can point higher. However, this is only effective in smooth water conditions. With the force generated by the sail also swinging sideways, forward power is reduced and the chances of separation magnify. In a chop, or anything rougher, it will be impossible to steer the boat sufficiently accurately to contain this.

Entry angle

In the earlier section on sailmaking the idea of adjusting the entry angle within the sail was introduced, again in relation to changing water conditions. Moving the maximum depth position forward allows a more forgiving shape, but pointing ability is sacrificed.

There are a number of trim options open to the sailor.

For rough water where it is impossible to accurately maintain the boats heading, the basic method is to crack the sheet and slightly bear off a few degrees to power through the waves. Not only does the whole sail move forward, the tension on the luff, now with proportionally greater effect in relation to that from the sheet, will pull the draft forward. Cracking the sheet will also increase twist. Good in stronger winds, but maybe a waste of potential power in anything lighter.

Moving the sheet lead forward will produce a similar entry angle, but will reduce twist and the depth-to-chord ratio will increase. This results in more lift but in anything other than light airs the chances of separation, with its associated drag, rise rapidly.

The third method is to allow the forestay to sag. Forestay sag is controlled either by backstay tension on a masthead rig or by the running backstays on a fractional rig. In difficult pointing conditions, when footing is preferable to keeping the boat on a knife edge, a controlled amount of sag in the forestay will allow the entry angle to deepen and make the sail more forgiving.

Its use with highly structured sails is very common. The more structured or rigid the fabric, the less halyard tension is necessary to position maximum camber depth. Allowing sag to develop in the forestay, whilst maintaining tension on the sail luff, edges maximum depth forward in a very controlled manner. Unfortunately, headstay sag also increases depth-to-chord ratio and reduces twist, particularly aloft. Sails made from the more structured

On the right, a small amount of headstay sag has pulled the max camber position forward, from its mid-chord position in the sail on the left.

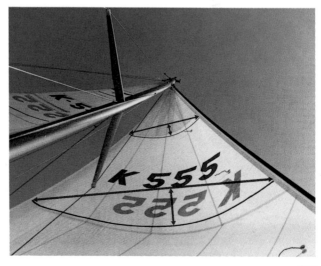

In very light airs, the headsail sheet lead is moved forward and inboard and the sheet eased. A parallel slot with the flattened mainsail is impossible.

fabrics require the sheet lead moved aft when the wind pipes up.

In less structured sails maximum draft position can be controlled, in conjunction with any of the above trim techniques, by halyard or luff Cunningham tension.

The rules again are simple. In anything other than rough seas, the optimum position for maximum camber is on or slightly forward of mid-chord. This gives high pointing ability but a narrow groove. Moving it forward widens the groove and makes it more forgiving, but at the expense of not being able to point high.

The position of maximum camber can only be accurately gauged from in front of the mast looking up into the top third of the sail. The perspective lower down, or from the helming position, is always distorted.

Fifth gear tell-tales

There is one final indication of precise entry angle. It is popular on highly competitive boats as a pointer to the helmsman that the headsail luff is trimmed to the optimum and the boat is pointing as high as possible.

At mid luff height a horizontal row of tell-tales are fitted leading right into the luff. Those on the leeward side indicate the existence of a separation bubble caused by too narrow an angle of attack.

By progressively easing the boat to windward, an expert helmsman can make first the aft tell-tale and subsequently those right at the luff stream aft. The trick is to keep them all streaming without fluttering any of the windward tell-tales ranged up and down the luff. A rounder luff entry eases the challenge, but it is in association with a fine entry and high pointing that they have earned the name of 'fifth-gear speedometer'.

The slot

So far the relationship between the leech of the headsail and the forward shape within the mainsail has been ignored. Time therefore to move attention aft.

In anything other than very light airs, twist in the leech of the headsail should parallel the adjacent vertical curve of the main, and vice versa. In very slow wind speeds this is not desirable. The foresail clew should be moved well forward and inboard, and the boat taken off the wind to a point where the windward tell-tales will stream. At the same time the main sheet should be eased, but the sail flattened.

That apart, what indications are to hand signifying an efficient slot? Remember the aim is to make it as easy as possible for leeward flow, slowing down as it nears the headsail leech, to be re-energised by the faster low pressure flow accelerating over the lee of the main. By making it too easy with too narrow a gap, this same low pressure flow off the main will be slowed by the relative high pressure to windward of the headsail. When that to leeward of the main slows to the same speed as the flow to windward, pressure on either side of the sail equalises, and the luff backwinds. Here then is the clue to slot width.

In almost all cases, if the tell-tales up and down the headsail luff are in step and maximum camber position at or forward of mid chord, headsail twist will be alright. Trimming can therefore be concentrated on matching the mainsail to this curve.

Slot width will be at its opti-

Beating into a good breeze, the slot in this fractional rig is parallel from top to bottom, and just wide enough to stop the flattened mainsail from being permanently backwinded.

mum when, or just before, the mainsail backwinds. Assuming that the athwartship headsail sheeting angle is positioned for the prevailing conditions, to reduce excessive backwinding will require the mainsail to be brought to windward to widen the slot. This will alter the balance of the boat, so an alternative has to be considered. (The same will apply if the slot is too wide, i.e. no sign of backwinding, calling for the main to be eased to leeward.)

The alternative is to flatten, or reduce the depth-to-chord ratio within the main and thereby alter the width of the slot. Not only are the controls available to do this, they are available also to control the relative width at any vertical height.

First the depth-to-chord ratio. In the lower third of the sail this is controlled by the clew outhaul. Increasing the distance between clew and tack will also flatten the upper chords in an unstructured fabric mainsail. Increasing mast bend is much more effective on the upper two-thirds of the main-sail, whatever the material.

By judicial adjustment of either or both, the main can be flattened until backwinding lifts the luff evenly throughout the height of the slot. This will of course be proportionally less for a fractional rig than for a masthead version. Any reluctance of the main to backwind calls for a reversal of all of the above. The sail can be deepened to reduce the slot using the same controls in reverse

Cunningham tension

Any change in tension across the horizontal chord will have to

be balanced with a corresponding adjustment to those running vertically. In other words maximum depth of camber must be correctly positioned.

In the case of structured sails, Cunningham is also used to iron out any creases running diagonally up into the sail from the clew. These are caused by mast bend during the sail flattening process.

Optimum draft position follows closely the rules laid down for the headsail, except that in light winds the maximum camber can be allowed to drift back to aft of mid chord.

It could by now be argued that both sails are trimmed, both as individuals and as a total aerofoil. A reasonable argument indeed, but here is the rub.

Unfortunately, those controls which shape the main have both a primary effect and secondary effect. Inevitably the secondary effect will have altered the shape of the mainsail leech and the original balance. Even had they not, the mainsail will now be working so effectively that its upwash effect on the foresail will

have freed the apparent wind. The foresail will need retrimming; and so on, and so on, and ...

Hopefully, for all but the most addicted sail trimmers, the foregoing provides sufficient on the concept, highlighting as it does, the most easily judged indicators. Sailing is after all supposed to be recreational.

The mast is progressively bent (from left to right) to flatten the mainsail and reduce backwinding in the slot to leeward.

Spinnakers

Downwind sailing is something of a paradox. In theory it should be the most mentally and physically relaxing of all points of progress. As was earlier noted, even a soldier should be in his element.

Unfortunately in practice it seems rarely as idyllic as it should. Progress in the reduced apparent wind is slow, and with the wind well aft the mainsail-shadowed headsail is the very devil to trim. Even when coaxed to set for more than a few moments at a time, the boat's narrow sheeting base effectively decimates its driving power.

Virtually all drive downwind is generated by the mainsail held out, across the airstream, by its boom. As was described earlier this force is almost wholly drag. Both the luff and leech of the mainsail now provide edges to the oncoming flow, but the extreme angle of attack at each is too great to coax the wind around onto the lee surface of the sail. It separates, and vortices are formed across the entire leeward surface. Meanwhile pressure builds on the windward surface adding to the forward force on the sail.

Working in the lee of the mainsail and its separated jumble of flow, the headsail is impossible to set effectively. One answer is to pole the clew out into clear flow on the opposite side to the boom. In other words, goosewinging the sail.

A more effective answer would be to boom out the tack of the headsail. In this way flow will meet the luff first, and the sheeting angle of the sail will be effectively increased. Incidentally, this is recognised by those familiar with it, as an extremely efficient and controllable rig for downwind sailing in very heavy weather.

Be that as it may, this easily understood concept is all that lies behind the development of the spinnaker, and its offspring commonly called the cruising chute.

Both the shape of the spinnaker and the material it is made out of are quite different to any headsail. These factors are merely developments along the road to efficiency. At heart the running spinnaker is a headsail, set with a flying luff from a pole extending it out into undisturbed flow.

Running

Early development moved towards a symmetrical shape largely due to handling problems. As the size of downwind, poled-out headsails grew, so did problems of gybing acres of canvas.

A full size genoa set as a spinnaker with the *tack* poled out to windward.

Photo: Nick Rains/PPL

It also became apparent that adding wider sections to the upper part of the sail significantly increased drive. This was in part due to the reduced influence of the mainsail as it narrowed towards its apex. There is however, another factor which may not have been quite so well realised at the time.

So far the concept of flow has been across sails in a vertical plane. However, a large and efficient edge of the spinnaker—that across its head, from shoulder to shoulder—meets downwind flow across a near horizontal plane. The extra efficiency comes from the reduced angle of attack where these meet, allowing the flow to be coaxed down over the leeward surface and generating lift. Not only does the lift supplement the drag forces working in the direction of travel, it raises the sail up and out, away in effect from the separated flow on the lee of the mainsail.

Aerodynamics

Reverting for a moment to aerodynamic theory, what are the forces on a spinnaker running before the wind?

In the top illustration shown from above, the sail is directly across the wind. The stagnation point occurs somewhere in the centre of the windward side of the sail, and the air flow either side of this splits, heading for a way out and around. At the edges it separates, forming swirling vortices which drag the sail and boat forward.

However, there is a tendency for the flow deflected from the windward curve to continue

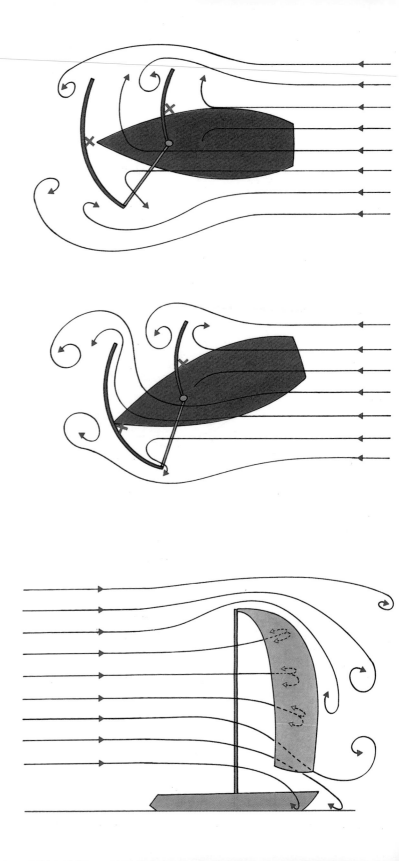

138

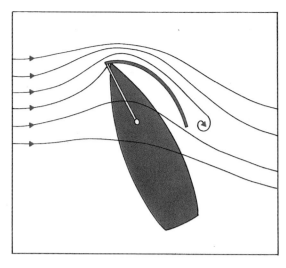

On a tight reach under spinnaker, partial separation is inevitable...
◄

...there is no way that flow will bend around the lee of a depth-to-chord ratio as great as this.
▼

spinnaker shape was dictated by the need for an effective downwind sail. The temptation to continue to use its massive area as the wind swung forward can be sympathised with. However, as the wind moves forward, or the boat points up, a fundamental change takes place. Now the spinnaker becomes like a conventional headsail. As the angle of attack at the luff reduces in relation to the flow, the flow reverts to the more familiar horizontal direction across the sail.

sideways before moving downwind. In effect it is increasing the area of the sail by adding a border around the edges. A smooth camber increases this effect and consequently the drag force on the sail.

In the centre diagram the sail has been angled 10–15 degrees off. The noticeable difference is that a small proportion of the flow meeting the luff remains attached onto the leeward surface due to the reduced angle of attack. The border effect on the luff has virtually disappeared, but has increased at the leech.

The third diagram (bottom) shows what is happening from the side. Quite a large proportion of flow remains attached to the leeward surface at the head creating significant lift. Some of this flow is deflected downwards, and in smooth conditions the effect of this can be seen as a slight rippling on the water below the spinnaker foot.

Reaching

The evolution of the basic

Viewed from above there is little difference between the flow pattern being generated over the spinnaker and that over a very full headsail. Taken to extremes however, as for example on a tight reach, some 50 per cent of the flow will separate, dragging the boat sideways. The depth-to-chord ratio is simply too large.

How the shape of the spinnaker or cruising chute can be manipulated, or trimmed, to counter these quite different flow patterns will hopefully become clear later. Suffice at this stage to understand some of the criteria which have to be met in design and construction of the sail.

Fabric

Although the concept of a running sail set flying goes back into the mists of time, the spinnaker of today is a comparatively recent development. Its brief story is closely woven with that of nylon, and specifically that developed for parachutes.

The properties sought after for parachutes and spinnakers are after all very similar. Lightweight, strength, elasticity to absorb shock loadings, controlled porosity and a degree of resistance to distortion all play a role in both end products.

Weight is one of the keys. Both headsails and mainsails benefit from support by the rig. The only support for the spinnaker on the other hand comes from those aerodynamic forces it generates by itself. All-purpose spinnakers for boats between 30

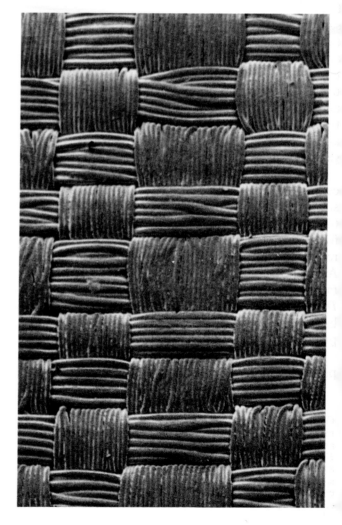

and 40 feet (LOA) would typically be made from 0.85 oz nylon. This compares with 5 or 6 oz *Dacron* for a full size headsail. Ounce for ounce nylon and *Dacron* are similar in strength, although nowhere near in terms of stretch or stability.

Nylon has in fact a number of additional interesting qualities which make it ideal for spinnakers and cruising chutes. The fine denier yarns are bulkier, weight for weight, than those of *Dacron*. The interstices formed during weaving are reduced even before heat treatment. This combination severely cuts down the porosity of the finished fabric, restricting the amount of flow which can seep through. The addition of polyurethane coatings make it virtually impermeable—at least when the spinnaker is new. Coatings also help to lock the weave together, reducing bias stretch.

The shock loadings experienced when a spinnaker fills in a strong wind are enormous. As they are prone to collapse and refill, these loadings are a fairly regular part of a spinnaker's life. A sail made of a less elastic material, such as for example *Dacron*, would require a rig and handling gear of truly massive proportions.

While polyurethane coating is popular, others including mel-

This laminate film spinnaker appeared in the forcing-house atmosphere of the 1987 America's Cup. *Photo: Barry Pickthall*

amine are also used to give more structure to the fabric. These add to the stability of the sail but are prone to break down from the nylon base. Because the sail design takes account of this extra stability, once the coating does break down, it will be far less satisfactory than one made from a fabric with a more flexible finish.

Tears are another problem directly related to the hardness of the finish. The lattice-like network of darker lines throughout spinnaker fabric comes from thicker and therefore stronger yarns incorporated during weaving. Commonly known as ripstop, their purpose is to stop small tears spreading. That is the theory, but in practice it has to be a very small tear for them to have any effect. However, when nylons with a softer finish are subjected to a sharp edge the yarns tend to

On the left, unfinished spinnaker nylon magnified × 80. The individual filaments are weight for weight, bulkier than *Dacron*, and the (horizontal) warp yarns are straighter. On the right, after heat setting and dyeing, the weave has tightened up. The thicker vertical yarn (centre), is part of a rip-stop square.

141

bunch together, sharing the load. A tear is much more difficult to start in the first place. Yarns held apart by a harder finish tend to break individually giving the tear a much easier foothold.

Shape

Modern spinnaker shape and design are both compromises aimed at the impossible. As has been seen, the optimum depth-to-chord ratio of a spinnaker running is very different from that which will allow it to act as an effective reaching sail. While running, a ratio of around 1 to 4 would catch the downwind flow very effectively. On a reach a practical ratio would be more in the region of 1 to 7.

The sail also has to be symmetrical. Although this does not apply to the cruising chute version, the true spinnaker has to provide the sailor with identical characteristics on either downwind tack.

A major consideration has to be stability, not only within the structure of the sail, but in its flying characteristics. Supported as it is at just three points, the shape has to be such that a high degree of equilibrium has to be achieved between those points and the forces generated by, and within, the sail.

One of the limiting factors faced by the designer is the relatively short foot with which he must work. If the sail is to be flattened effectively for reaching and

The upper part of a spinnaker should ideally conform to the surface of a perfect sphere.

yet a degree of control on the upper power-producing region is to be maintained while running, the foot and lower chords must be narrow.

Most critical, for this jack-of-all-trades sail, the full head must be capable of being opened at will if the sail is not to heel the boat over on a reach.

The answers are not easy. Compounded indeed by the widely admitted gaps in the knowledge of all sailmakers on the finer points of how a running spinnaker actually works. The problem here lies with the almost total absence of any scientific comparative data on the subject. Neither does it appear that this condition is likely to change. Surface lifting theory data does not exist for such shapes, and the problems of plotting stress and generated force appear insurmountable to many experts. Even the ubiquitous computer has problems unravelling the variables fed in from moulded and membrane shape concepts.

Spinnaker shape is therefore almost totally the result of the empirical approach. Theory is tried out, and, tempered with experience, the results are refined further.

Mathematically the head and upper part of the sail is fairly straightforward. To maximise every possible square foot of area the theoretical ideal will correspond closely to the outer suface of a sphere. Peeling an orange gives a good idea of the principle.

The universal consensus from empirical refinement is that an elliptical cross section offers the best practical compromise to cope with a wide range of wind speeds and sailing angles. This is the running shape which, with the right construction, and understanding trim, can best be adapted to an efficient reaching section.

Relative flatness across the centre of the sail maximises power whilst running, and the rather greater camber at each edge improves sail stability. On a reach the leech can be flattened into a reasonable aerofoil.

Empirical developments in shape naturally run hand in hand with progress in materials and construction. Neither moves very far ahead without the other. The evolution in spinnaker construction is therefore worth looking at next.

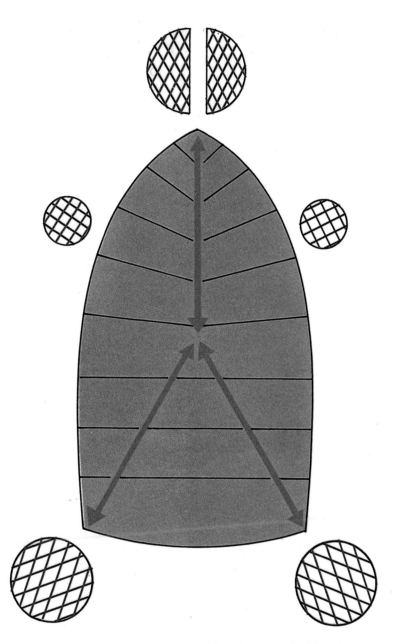

Construction

Until the early sixties spinnakers were made from two identical halves, the nylon panels in each side being simply sewn horizontally together with no attempt at individually shaping each edge. The sail took its shape from an early version of vertical broad-seaming of its central seam where the two halves were sewn together. Unfortunately the resultant curves were neither horizontally nor vertically fair. Camber was particularly deep up and down the central seam, and at its most acute at the head.

More important however, the Stretch across the bias, from the three corners and along the upper vertical seam, in a cross-cut spinnaker, is unequal to that along the threadline of either leech.

cross cut, both in this early version and in more sophisticated developments a full decade later, displayed a less than ideal orientation of old friends, warp and fill.

143

Stresses resulting from the force generated by a spinnaker radiate out from the body of the sail to the three attachment points at head, tack and clew. In a cross cut spinnaker those heading for tack and clew line up across the weaker bias of the fabric. The load towards the head follows the seam joining panels cut on the bias to form the top of the sail. Resistance to stretch, particularly in this latter area, was much less than that along the edges of the sail, supported by fill yarns.

On a run, this distortion as the wind increased, simply led to a fuller sail section. The edges adjacent to the lower attachment points collapsed in towards the centre of the sail, adding fullness to the lower sections. This was fine, but the more unyielding fill yarns following leech and luff at the head drew the edges together, increasing the depth-to-chord ratio aloft. It was not ideal, but on a run the cross-cut was livable-with.

On a reach, with its accompanying increase in apparent wind, it would be quite a different matter. The real problem then lay high in the sail, increasing separation, drag and heeling moment. Camber in the foot could to a degree be reduced by tension on the sheet, but this had little or no effect on the sail aloft. For reaching the cut was impracticable.

Radial head

This concern with reaching performance led to the introduction of the radial head spinnaker. To counteract distortion in the

upper part of the sail, the cross cut cloth was replaced with a series of narrow tapered panels radiating down from the head, and so spreading the load. Each radial panel was cut with the warp threadline running through its length, thereby dramatically improving the stability at the top of the sail.

The late Bruce Banks' *Windsprite*, demonstrating a perfect running shape with a radial head spinnaker.

Interestingly, the nylon used for spinnakers is always warp orientated. That is, the warp yarns stretch less than those across the fill of the fabric; the opposite in fact to the weave of conventional *Dacron*. It is a limitation due to

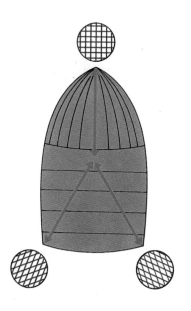

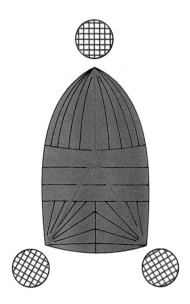

Radial head construction (top left) solved the critical head shaping challenge by orienting panels, and (red) warp yarns, fanwise from the head. The tri-radial (right) took this idea a stage further, with similar 'fans' coming into the sail from the lower corners as well.

The radial head construction is less satisfactory on a reach. The sail is too deep, and the leech is closed.

nylon weaving which cannot, apparently, be overcome.

Whilst moving some way towards an answer for reaching, the radial head improved also the quality of the spinnaker when running. This is well demonstrated in the picture (far left). At the head the sail has lifted into a beautifully fair curve which extends from the horizontal right down to the vertical at mid depth. This has been matched by a degree of collapse in the lower, cross-cut half of the sail. The convex curve along the foot has disappeared up into the body of the sail, and the leech has become concave. The body of the sail could be said to have blossomed.

Whilst the radial head was in reaching terms an improvement on the cross-cut, it represented only the first step on the ladder. When reaching in anything but the lightest breeze, very little control over fullness could be exerted from the bottom corners.

Starcut

One answer, developed in the mid-sixties by the Bruce Banks loft on the south coast of England, not only gave sailors the reaching spinnaker they yearned for, but pointed the way forward for every sailmaker in the world.

By extending the radial head principle for all three corners with panels radiating fan-wise into the body of the sail, designer Ken Rose was for the first time able to exert control over the whole of the spinnaker. Each panel was cut to take maximum advantage of the unyielding warp threadlines. The cut of each panel was also dictated by spherical geometry. An extremely complex set of calculations was necessary for each sail.

Depth-to-chord ratios throughout these flat-cut reaching spinnakers could be controlled with sheet tension by simply increasing or reducing the distance between tack and clew.

The position of maximum camber could be adjusted as easily as in a headsail, by altering the height of the spinnaker pole in the same way that halyard tension is used to move camber in a conventional headsail.

Such was the breakthrough that a year after the Starcut first appeared in 1967, the then captain of the British Admirals' Cup team insisted that each skipper in the squad acquire at least one for the coming competition.

145

Tri-radial panelling is obvious in the striking red and white design.

Tri-radial

The Starcut represented, in a sense, a move away from the idea of compromise in spinnaker design. To be competitive each boat required at least two spinnakers, a radial head for running and a Starcut for reaching. The extra cost, and added effort in having to change sails, weighed against the concept.

Cost also obviated any real effort to harness the Starcut idea to an all-purpose spinnaker. The sophisticated geometry of the panel layout was, for the period, expensive enough in the Banks' sail with its origins in a clever computer programme. For other sailmakers reproducing the design each time on the loft floor, it was prohibitive. Interestingly, 20 years on there are signs that an all-purpose sail of very similar concept may be the way foward, but at the time the thrust was towards an economic and practical 'best of both worlds' compromise. The result was the tri-radial.

At the head, the all important orange peel spherical shape is formed by a series of radial panels. Distortion of the moulded shape is minimised as the loads within, and along each edge of the spinnaker, closely follow the warp threadline of each fabric panel.

The radial panels in the bottom corners also minimise the effect of load from the clew and tack attachment points, although here the aim is to maintain a

vertically flat section. Early radial corners, and some still made today, were made from panels with completely straight edges. Because the loads radiating up into the sail are greatest in the middle of each corner, these lead to hard ridges developing up into the body of the sail. Better tri-radials today have a degree of shaping in each corner panel to spread the loads more evenly.

In the centre of the sail the horizontal panels actually help the sail to 'blossom'. Most of the loads from the three corners have

noted, one route is to radially shape panels throughout the sail. Another is to align the warp orientated nylon vertically along the load lines between the head radials and those from each corner in a series of 'square-cut' panels. A further development still is to rock these central panels, aligning the warp threads even more directly along the load lines. It goes without saying, that all increase the necessary depth-to-chord ratio of the sailor's pocket.

Panels in the cross-cut mid-section of this tri-radial spinnaker have been vertically 'rocked' to align warp yarns between the radial head and corner sections. *Photo: Barry Pickthall* ▼

Sheet tension has caused hard creases to form from clew corners of both these spinnakers. This is known as clew inversion.

been dissipated by the time they reach the mid-height, and the relative instability of the cross threadline panels acts as flexible mounting between the three more stable corners. A degree of bias-stretch in the centre is also helpful in rounding the leading edge of the spinnaker and thereby increasing stability of the whole sail.

Computer aided design has allowed the sailmaker to look again at this middle, cross-cut section to meet demands made by the all-out racing fraternity, and as was

Nylon spinnaker panels are cut to shape using a heated roller knife which melts and seals the fabric edge.

Spinnaker making

The early stages of making a spinnaker are quite different from those employed for a fore and aft sail. The eventual spherical shape is impractical to mark out on the loft floor, so the sail designer must resort to a more mathematical approach. From the basic dimensions of height and mid-girth width the number, shape and sizes of each panel, both radial and cross-cut, can be calculated using the formula in favour at the time. In most cases the panels within each of the four sections, the head, centre and both corners, will be identical, although some of the radials towards the edge of a spinnaker may differ. The panels for asymmetrical cruising chutes are more often cut to an outline on the loft floor, although any radial sections will be calculated as above.

The spinnaker panels are then cut to shape in stacks, or layers, of up to six at a time using a hot knife. This is a heated wheel with a sharp edge which when rolled along the nylon, melts and seals the edge of the fabric. The panels in each of the four sections are then sewn together.

From this point, shaping and final assembly more closely follow conventional sailmaking techniques. The edges along which each section meets its neighbour are critical to the eventual shape of the sail. Each joining edge must be broadseamed and this is done by laying out the sections on the loft floor and cutting in the prescribed curves.

Once the four sections are

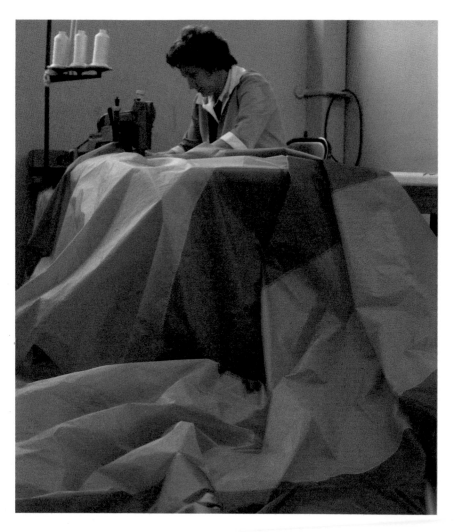

around which the curve is formed. The rest of the curve, individual to each sailmaker, will aim to maximise sail area without compromising luff stability.

Large patches, each layer staggered in size, are added to each corner to spread the load into the radial panels. Finally the edges are taped. As with leech tabling, the relative tensions of sail and tape during this latter operation are critical. If the tabling is tensioned too much the luff and leech will hook. Equally, because the luff particularly depends on the tape for its flying stability, too little original tension will result in a luff which is difficult to make stand.

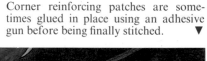

Corner reinforcing patches are sometimes glued in place using an adhesive gun before being finally stitched. ▼

Seaming a larger spinnaker is a lengthy job.

joined together, the sail must return again to the loft floor for final shaping of the vertical edges, or in the case of the cruising chute, the luff and leech. In both cases this is done, as with a fore and aft sail, using long battens bent around prickers stuck into the loft floor. As the size of spinnakers is almost always dictated by a racing rule limiting the mid-girth dimension, this will be the fulcrum

Spinnaker trim

Enough could be written about spinnaker trim to fill a book on its own. Equally, the basics, upon which the more esoteric techniques depend, are little understood. These revolve around the simple concept that, although a spinnaker may look very different, it is controlled and reacts in exactly the same manner as a conventional headsail.

First of all, whether reaching or running, the luff has to be presented to the prevailing wind flow at the correct angle of attack. Too great and flow will separate behind the leading edge forming a bubble; too little and flow and therefore pressure will remain equal over both surfaces luffing the leading edge. There are two differences between the spinnaker luff and that of a headsail. One is that the former must stand alone, unsupported by a forestay. The second is that it can be moved in relation to the boat.

With the pole-end, and tack, across the wind, the angle of attack of the sail's leading edge becomes a function of the sheet in exactly the same way as it does for any other headsail. However, while tell-tales will indicate horizontal flow patterns while reaching, downwind they just confuse matters.

The only indication that the angle of attack is too narrow is a collapse of the luff. It curls, or folds in on itself. The correct angle must therefore be just before that point. If the spinnaker luff is not trimmed to the point where curl is regularly apparent,

then too great a proportion of the total force being generated will be across the direction of travel.

In the vertical plane the sheet also controls the relative angle of attack up and down the luff. If the sheet lead is too far forward the whole spinnaker tilts aft at the head and the lower leading edge luffs. Too far aft, and the converse happens; camber in the upper luff deepens, the angle of attack is effectively reduced and the sail curls in. The big difference of course is that the tack of the spinnaker, by adjusting the pole height, can also be raised and lowered, with a consequently similar effect on the trailing edge of the leech.

When running, the pole/tack height is used to balance out the tilting effect of the sheet and at the same time, raise the sail to its optimum height in the prevailing wind.

If the luff folds first near the head, raise the pole. If the lower luff collapses first, lower the pole. A modern tri-radial spinnaker should curl first just above the cross-cut panels. This is a much better method of judging the correct pole height then the old wisdom of keeping tack and clew equal. Too often this is distorted by sheet tension keeping the clew low.

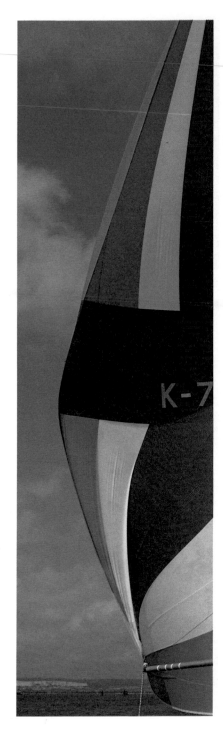

Far left, the pole is low relative to the clew, and the luff folds near the head. In the centre, the tack (pole) has been raised, and the fold is nearer mid-luff. In the right hand picture, it has been raised too high, resulting in the lower luff curling first.

151

With the pole high and sheet lead aft, the shoulders of the spinnaker open (top). Compare the depth-to-cord ratio with that below, where the pole has been lowered and the sheet lead taken forward.

nent from the sheet by moving it aft, and balancing this with pole height allows the sail aloft to spread its wings for maximum power. Conversely, when the wind increases and the sail needs to be de-powered, moving the sheet lead forward, and the pole down, will narrow the sail aloft.

The rough rule of thumb for pole angle on a run is to have it close to 90 degrees across the apparent wind. However once the wind is well aft this squaring of the pole increases the chord in the lower half of the spinnaker. Not only is that area of the sail flattened, the angle of attack of the lower luff is greatly increased and the whole spinnaker brought closer to the bubble of separated flow downwind of the mainsail. Ease the pole forward therefore to keep the depth-to-chord ratio constant with that higher in the sail.

Another good guide to pole angle is to keep the vertical centre seam of the sail parallel to the mast. If the seam slopes to leeward aloft ease the pole forward, and vice versa.

Staying on a run, the downward component from the sheet has again exactly the same effect on the upper leech as it does on a headsail. Too much and the leech closes, increasing the depth-to-chord ratio. In a spinnaker, lowering the pole mirrors this effect on the luff. Both edges of the sail aloft are brought together narrowing the chord.

As was seen, the aim on a run is to present as wide a sail area as possible to the following wind. Reducing the downward compo-

152

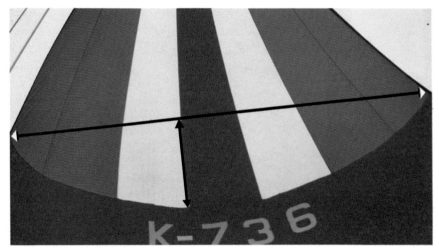

On a reach, the maximum camber position will remain at mid-chord (top) unless the pole is lowered in relation to the clew (below). The deeper forward camber is more forgiving, and the leech has opened.

Reach trim

Once reaching, as was seen, the spinnaker more closely approximates to a very full headsail, with flow now moving horizontally across its surfaces. Tell-tales positioned in the luff areas of

The angle made between spinnaker halyard and the forestay/wind indicator (left) shows most effort from the sail is sideways. Easing the sheet by a couple of feet on this Half-Ton size boat, has moved the halyard (and sail) much closer to the direction of travel (right).

the cross cut panelling work effectively as indicators of sheet tension, although most sailors stick to trimming by luff curl.

The position of maximum camber depth now takes on a significant role. Again the same principle as with a conventional headsail applies. Lowering the pole increases the distance between head and tack of the sail. Maximum camber moves forward and the leech flattens allowing flow to exit efficiently from both surfaces. Too little relative tension on the luff gives a fine entry and a sideways drag-producing leech. Exactly what is not needed to keep the boat on its feet. However, too much tension on the luff will also close the upper leech in a radial head construction, so pole height when close reaching is a fine judgement.

One final indicator is worth watching as the reach gets closer and closer. The angle that the halyard makes with the centre line is an absolutely perfect indication of the direction of total force generated by the spinnaker.

It is amazing how marked an effect a slight easing of the sheet, or a pull back on the pole, will have on the degree by which the halyard swings forward. Angled at anything greater than 45 degrees to the direction of travel and it is time for the sail to be replaced by a headsail.

153

A cruising chute of quite sophisticated construction (above) sets well tacked down to the stem head. A closer look (right) reveals that, despite a flat sea, the mainsail is heavily reefed to give the chute a clear following wind.

Cruising chutes

Spinnakers are blessed with appalling public relations. Their association with racing does absolutely nothing to endear them to a cruising sailor, particularly as some of the best photographs depict them when things have gone

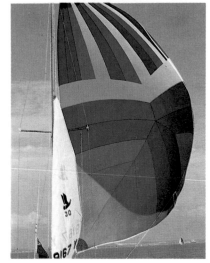

awry. The boat is out of control, on its ear, and thousands of square feet of nylon are thrashing at the tethers.

Sadly racing does that to spinnakers. They get overpressed and hit back. Spinnakers used for cruising on the other hand are models of virtue. Their only purpose is downwind in light to moderate airs. In anything heavier, the main will do the job unaided. One of the axioms of the late Bruce Banks was that too many sailors missed the best bit; sailing downwind in flat seas and a following breeze. All too often lack of progress and a flapping headsail ends in the engine being switched on.

Be that as it may, the need for a more efficient, easily handled light downwind sail led to another compromise; the cruising chute. Originally conceived as a halfway house, which looked like a spinnaker but which was as handy as a headsail, the end hardly lived up to the promise.

In effect the cruising chutes were little more than large light-weight overlapping genoas. Extended luffs, sometimes made even longer by tack pennants, allowed them to be set flying, free of the forestay. Set to leeward of the main and with the inevitable lack of sheeting angle, the sail suffered much the same setting problems as a large headsail on anything approaching a run.

The asymmetrical design derives from attempts to harden the leech and add fullness to the sail, at the same time as raising the height of the clew. Both, in theory, help the sail to blossom out ahead of the mainsail. In practice the shadow thrown by the latter calls for constant sheet trim which goes some way to defeating the object of the exercise.

To really work effectively, the cruising chute, like any other headsail downwind, has to be tacked out in relatively clear flow. This means a pole and most of the other gear associated with the labour intensive spinnaker.

The argument then for a spinnaker gathers momentum. If the gear needed is equal, then the spinnaker is more efficient; is just as easy (or hard) to hoist, and more importantly take down; and because it is symmetrical, can be gybed as the wind goes by the lee.

A cruising chute tacked to the stem can be gybed, but if tacked out on a pole the sail has to be lowered and flown again on the other side of the boat.

Spinnaker socks

One idea more than any other has dispelled apprehension about taming both spinnaker and cruising chute for the short-crewed crusing sailor. The spinnaker sock is a luff-length nylon tube with a rigid plastic bell-shaped mouth at one end which literally swallows the sail from the head downwards, smothering its wilder tendencies as it comes.

The sail is hoisted already in the sock. Once sheet and guy are bent to clew and tack, the bell-mouth is raised on its own separate halyard, releasing the spinnaker. To douse the sail, either the sheet or guy is first eased and the mouth pulled down by its control line, swallowing the sail.

This, plus the realisation by the cruising sailor that hoisting and taking down a spinnaker are actions that can be taken when circumstances are at the optimum, add up to a persuasive argument for having a go.

Ninety per cent of spinnaker handling problems on racing boats occur because the sail has to be hoisted and lowered when the race, rather than the sailor, dic-

A spi-sock in action (left to right), effectively smothering a cruising chute. *Photo: Margherita Bottini/courtesy North Sails.*

tates. The cruiser can take his own time, with the wind aft and the spinnaker shadowed. Neither does he have to keep it aloft for one moment longer than prudence favours.

Big boy/blooper

The big boy/shooter/blooper, which first appeared in the early 1970s owes its origins to a simple desire by racing sailors for extra downwind sail area. A light *Dacron* headsail tacked via a strop to the bow was flown clear to leeward of both spinnaker and mainsail by only half hoisting the halyard.

Nylon constructions soon followed in a variety of cuts designed to encourage the sail to fly both outward and upward. So extended is the halyard, the only force keeping a well set big-boy out of the water is that self-generated laterally, deflecting the halyard to leeward.

Its debut was greeted with cries of 'unseamanlike', but ironically it has been its contribution in that very area that has kept it alive.

Spinnakers flown in heavier airs downwind induce rolling. Uncorrected, and this calls for a bold and deft hand on the tiller, these oscillations deepen and accelerate into what is aptly termed a 'death-roll'. A by-product of the big-boy is that it adds an extra stabilising factor to one side of the boat, rather like that which an outrigger gives to a proa. The tendency to roll is substantially reduced.

It should be clearly under-

stood however, just how the big-boy should be flown. It is designed to extend the area of the spinnaker out past the shadow of the mainsail and into clear air to leeward. Flow arriving first at the leech of the big-boy can be directed through the gap between its luff and the leech of the spinnaker, provided the auxiliary sail's luff is far enough forward. This calls for considerable amounts of ease on both halyard and sheet.

Without this the sail can easily do more harm than good. Whilst it may still look powerful, flow from leech to luff is directed into the slow moving high pressure area to windward of the spinnaker, reducing its effect.

The secret of effective big-boy flying, with halyard and sheet eased out, allowing the sail to set well clear of disturbed flow from the mainsail. *Photos: Dave Blunden.*

Index